KEEP YOUR LOVE ON!

CONNECTION, COMMUNICATION & BOUNDARIES

DANNY SILK

 TO MY CHOSEN SHERI

Endorsements for
Loving on Purpose Ministries

"*Keep Your Love On!* carries a timeless and undying message of God's unconditional love and wisdom in relationships. This message is particularly pertinent at a time when love is often understood as a feeling rather than a choice. Hope and healing will be released as you read this book. Read it individually, read it with your family, read it in a group, but read it! Many have been touched and changed."

Barry & Lori Byrne
REDDING, CA

"Author Danny Silk does an incredible job of equipping you to finally build the relationships you've hoped for. His stories create laughter, his relational insight astounds you, but most importantly his message is full of catalytic empowerment for your life! Who on earth doesn't desire to love and be loved really well? After a decade of ministry in the area of relationships, we can honestly say that Danny Silk's material on building connection and healthy communication is at the top of our list of resources! This book is packed with powerful, practical and solid insight for creating healthy connected relationships. We highly recommend it to singles and couples alike!"

Josh & April LaFrance
REDDING , CA

"The light was turned on to practical truth....We no longer expect perfection or demand obedience, but instead cherish our relationships. I can manage myself in the presence of sin without turning my love off and my kids are learning to clean up their own messes!"

Amy Vitacolonna
HOUSTON, TX

"I read *Loving Our Kids On Purpose* with the intention of becoming a better parent to my kids. Instead, I ended up better understanding my own childhood and why I am the way I am...I discovered some serious issues in my own life (like fear that had come from all the 'yellow trucking' my own parents had done to me), how it was affecting my own parenting, and how I needed to change. I have read the book three times and need to read it again. Thanks for all your encouragement and in helping me become whole."

Laurisa Myers
SHAWNEE, KANSAS

"*Loving Our Kids On Purpose* hasn't just impacted my family, but also my classroom. There is peace and fun in the midst of 27 children as we boot fear out of the classroom together. On the occasions when I am under pressure and step into my 'old style' of driving the children, they suggest that, 'I might like some time out!' I ask their forgiveness, we laugh together and move on. What joy and what freedom! I can see that anger only produces fear and no child, or adult for that matter, gives their best when they are fearful. So thank you, I always knew there had to be a better way...."

Rebecca Bouker
UK

"The biggest change in our home is the absence of fear. When you try to control someone (be it your kids, your husband, or your colleagues) you need some kind of leverage in order to get the required results. I had 'the stare,' 'the spoon,' 'the voice,' and a lot of frustration and anger. Throw those together, add a little power struggle, and you've not a nasty atmosphere with complete disconnect. When I realized that I was in agreement with the spirit of fear in order to get 'Christian' results of compliance, I knew I had grabbed the wrong end of the stick. I don't need that rod anymore now that we have kids and parents who are in control of themselves. There is an atmosphere of honor and love—and there is deep connection—even when life throws us curve balls."

Yannick Nel
SOUTH AFRICA

"Thank you Danny for this book, and thank you for being a man who stands for God's women! It hit me exactly where I am, and now I am starting to hear God's call on my life. Thank you for *Powerful & Free!*"

Hanna Matikainen
FINLAND

"As a foster parent with five kids in the house, *Loving Our Kids on Purpose* was a Godsend. God's heart for parents was revealed to me and I am forever thankful. It has changed not only my parenting, but also my relationships with my wife and family. I no longer walk around angry. I enjoy my kids and am so thankful for our heart to heart connection!"

Marcus Glascock
HANFORD, CA

"*Loving Our Kids on Purpose* led me to discover I had unresolved anger and guilt (causing my 3 year-old to fear me). Now, I've been healed. It has saved our relationship and broken the cycle of fear and dysfunction I grew up with. It saved my family. We know now what it is like to live in freedom! Thank you so much!"

Derrick Toh
SINGAPORE

CONTENTS

Introduction

Relationships are vital to becoming a whole person. I wrote this book to help people build, strengthen, and heal their relational connections. This has been my personal mission statement for the last 20 years.

As a husband, father, foster parent, group home staff member, social worker, program director, group facilitator, pastor, author, speaker, or leader, my goal has remained the same—I am alive to help people connect and stay connected.

Keep Your Love On is a mind-set. It is a heart condition. It's something no one can make you do and no one can keep you from doing. It is a force with a life of its own. Once this force begins to build momentum in your life, you will be able to love fully and do just about anything in life. Keeping your love on creates fearlessness and deep vulnerability.

The goal of life-long love is something everyone desires. It is the hope of every young couple who gaze into each other's eyes and believe that this is "The One." It is the commitment young parents make when they look into the innocent face of their first child. However, quality love relationships do not happen by accident. Real love is built the old-fashioned way—through hard work. And if you learn to manage the very best of who you are, the all-elusive intimacy experience we crave will be well within your grasp.

This book's arrangement is strategic. I know how important it is build one precept upon another. Three major relational themes are woven together to serve the goal of healthy relationships: connection, communication, and setting boundaries. These three relational components are familiar terms but seem to evade so many people when it comes to practicing and integrating them into their daily lives.

This book is not about "how to have good relationships in three easy steps." No, no, no. Relationships require a lot of effort from both sides if they are going to succeed. What I have done is simplified the basic principles of connecting, communicating, and setting boundaries, and I have laid out how to apply them through simple and learnable skills.

In these pages, you will find a fresh understanding of how powerful you are in forming lasting connections with others. You will learn how to keep your love on no matter what other people choose to do. Finding the right goals in communication will change your experience of conflict and disagreements. Understanding the process of lowering anxiety and increasing safety and care will lead you into places of trust and intimacy you thought were fantasies. Setting boundaries will allow you to take control of your time, energy, and resources in such a way that you can truly take care of your highest priorities and accomplish your mission and calling in life.

Day by day you will develop a plan to implement these new skills. You'll be able to think through and decide how you will respond in the next situation that challenges your connections, communication, or boundaries. My desire is for you to build the necessary skills to form healthy relationships. These skills come through purposeful practice.

Please know that this book is a culmination of decades of learning in my own life. I do not have any untested theories for you. I only have what has worked for me and for those I've helped over the years. I pray that you will find hope and healing in these pages. I am grateful that you are among those in the world today who are learning how to love well.

Peace,

Danny

Section One

CONNECTION

Chapter One

POWERFUL PEOPLE, POWERFUL RELATIONSHIPS

I t was June 16th, 1984—my wedding day. The main event had arrived at last.

Sheri, my bride, faced me as we stood between Pastor Bill Johnson and our guests, ready to pledge lifelong devotion and love to one another. Moments before, Bill and his wife, Beni, had sung a beautiful duet, preparing a perfect atmosphere for the exchange of solemn vows. Then Bill turned to me and began to ask the old, weighty questions, leading me through the promises to be faithful through sickness and health, for richer or poorer, till death do us part.

Finally, Bill asked me, "Do you choose Sheri as your wife for as long as you shall live?"

"I do."

Little did I know the significance of what I had just said. Like anyone else on his or her wedding day, I really had no idea what I was signing up for when I chose Sheri. Only as I journeyed through the first twelve years of our marriage, which challenged and invited me to hold to that choice again and again in the most difficult of circumstances, would I come to understand that speaking these words had ushered me into the test of a lifetime.

We echoed this language later in our wedding ceremony, when we exchanged rings. After I put the gold band on Sheri's finger, Bill asked me to repeat a further set of vows. "My chosen, Sheri," he began, "with this ring I commit my life to you…"

"My chosen, Sheri." To this day, I use this phrase to communicate my most intimate and devoted message to my wife. Every time she hears these three words, she lights up. It's as though I have pumped fresh blood into the connection we established on that day nearly thirty years ago, easing her anxieties and administering a life-giving dose of comfort, affection, and security to her heart. These words remind her that I not only chose her on our wedding day, but that I also continued to choose her, even through the rough early years of our marriage. Yes, there were times in those years—too many times—when I wrestled with that choice and how to play it out. I even considered going back on that choice on a few occasions. But each time, I returned to the words I had spoken. I now know that I will always do so, no matter what. I've signed numerous notes and cards with "My chosen, Sheri" to remind her of that choice— and to remind myself as well. Those words may have ushered me into the test of a lifetime, but they also brought me through it. Holding to them is what taught me to keep my love on.

A Faulty Foundation

"I choose you." This is the foundation of true, lasting relationships. It is the foundation for God's relationship with you. As Jesus declared to His disciples, "You did not choose Me, but I chose you…" [1] Jesus chose you in the most difficult of circumstances. He chose you while you were in sin, while you were His enemy. His side of the relationship with you does not depend upon your choice, but entirely upon His choice. The question is whether or not you will learn to build your relationships with Him and others upon the foundation of your choice.

Unfortunately, most people haven't learned to build their relationships on the premise, "I choose you." Their premise for relationship is, "You chose me." Take the typical high school lunchroom. On the first day of school, everyone enters the lunchroom with their brown paper bags and the weighty knowledge that their entire social status for the year is about to be determined by what happens in the next half hour. They scan the room, identify each group of people, and wonder which one they should join. *Hmm…I can't sit with the Goth kids because I'm not Goth. Could I be Goth? I like that they are quiet… But no, then I would have to wear black eyeliner all the time and I don't like black. Ooh, there are the cheerleaders. I like sports. But do the cheerleaders even know about the sports they are cheering for?*

This inner debate continues until someone yells out, "Hey you! Yes, you. Do you want to sit with us?" Relieved that someone is choosing them, they shut their brain off and wander over to the table where they will probably sit for the rest of the year.

It's simply our natural instinct to like people who like us and to choose people who choose us. This instinct even extends to non-humans. When a dog licks the face of its owner, the owner smiles and thinks, "I love this dog! Look at how much this dog loves me." His friends might think it is disgusting, but the dog owner enjoys being liked, even if he gets slobbered on.

However, if all our relationships are based solely on our natural impulse to return liking for liking, then we're going to have problems. Liking is a conditional state—it changes. Making "you chose me" the foundation of a relationship dooms it to change, and probably collapse, the minute one person's liking happens to turn south. I can see disaster coming from miles away when I meet with couples for pre-marriage counseling, ask the man to describe his bride-to-be, and hear something like this:

"Uh, she's hot. She loves me. I really love that she loves me. That is my favorite thing about her. She could have had any guy, but she chose me. I am so lucky."

I wish I could say such a response isn't common, but I can't. When nothing I hear tells me that a man is choosing a bride for her own sake, because she is the one he wants, I can say with a great deal of certainty that the relationship is fragile. What will happen when his wife stops showing him the same degree of affection she did when they were engaged? What happens if someone "hotter" comes along and decides to choose him?

A healthy, lasting relationship can only be built between two people who choose one another and take *full* responsibility for that choice. This choice must be based on who they are, what they want, and what they are committed to doing as individuals. Traditional marriage vows express the nature of this choice beautifully. The two people standing at the altar do not say, "You will. You will love me and cherish me in sickness and in health, till death do us part." And they don't say, "I will love you as long as you love me. I will be faithful to you as long as you are faithful to me." Their vows are all about what *they* are going to do. "I will love you. I will protect you. I will serve you. I will be faithful to you, no matter what."

In order to be able to make and keep commitments like this—commitments to enduring, intimate relationships—you need to be a certain kind of person. You need to be a *powerful* person. Powerful people take responsibility for their lives and choices. Powerful people choose who they want to be with, what they are going to pursue in life, and how they are going to go after it.

Unfortunately, most of us did not grow up to be powerful people. If you were blessed to have parents who taught you to be responsible for your choices, then you should go home and thank them. It's a rare gift. Most people don't know that they can be powerful, or even that they ought to be. They are trained from a young age that someone else is responsible for their decisions, and all they have to do is comply and obey. This sets them up to struggle in multiple aspects of life, particularly with building healthy relationships.

Powerless People

Often the first thing that reveals a powerless mindset is powerless language. Frequent use of the phrases "I can't" and "I have to" is a hallmark of a powerless person. "I can't do that. It's too hard. I have to clean the kitchen. I have to go to school. I have to spend time with so-and-so." All of these statements say, "I feel powerless to take responsibility for my actions, so I will say that someone or something else is making me do it."

Powerless people also throw in "I'll try" to absolve them if they do not come through on a commitment or promise. Just imagine standing in front of the preacher on your wedding day and saying, "I'll try." This language is rooted in powerlessness, in the belief that you don't have power to manage yourself.

The defining, driving force of a powerless person is anxiety. Life is scary when you are powerless, when you live in a world where you believe most things and most people are more powerful than you. It's scary to feel your life is out of your control.

Powerless people have a deep need to suppress and assuage their abiding fear—fear of loss, pain, death, abandonment, and more. But because they do not have the power deal with their fear, their only hope is to persuade other people to do it for them. They need other people to share their power with them, because they don't have any of their own. They *need* other people to protect them, make them happy, and take responsibility for their lives. And the only way they believe they can get people to do this is to try to control and manipulate them. Control can look aggressive like a T-Rex or passive like a lamb, but in either case, the root problem is the same—fear.

Powerless people approach relationships as consumers. They are always looking for other people who have resources of love, happiness, joy, and comfort to offer in a relationship to share with them, because they don't have any. They subconsciously think, *You look so happy. I need some of that happy in my life. We should get together so I can consume all of your happy.* A powerless person will consume whatever another person will offer up until the life of a once-happy, radiant flower has been mown to dirt. If you don't believe me, talk to anyone who has been in relationship with a powerless person. They will suck you dry—if you let them.

I have a friend who is married to a man with a debilitating victim mentality. She could never do enough and constantly struggled to live up to his impossible expectations. They recently separated because he refuses to take responsibility for his unhappiness. Since she has been on her own, she's like a flower getting sunshine for the first time. She's sleeping, losing weight, wearing makeup, and doing her hair. Her happiness is no longer being consumed by a powerless person.

Powerless people often blame the messes they make on other people. The reason their life, marriage, child, finances, job, or whatever is the way it is has nothing to do with their choices. Someone else—their parents, their spouse, their teachers, society—created the life they're living. They don't have the power to create their own lives.

Powerless people create an anxiety-driven environment wherever they go. At best, these environments have a thin veneer of safety and calm, which cover underlying currents of control and intimidation. Those who enter their atmosphere quickly learn to shape up and go with the program—until it dawns on them that they will never be safe to "just be themselves" around that person or group. Then they have a choice. Will they stay in the anxiety and submit to the control of the powerless people, or go looking for a different environment?

Many choose to stick around in controlling environments and develop the skills necessary to survive there. They acquire a bodysuit of anxiety-Kevlar, and then they live in it 24/7. It feels safe and impenetrable. The problem is that the armor shielding them from "scary" people is also preventing them from developing intimate connections with safe people. Their self-protection is not helping them become powerful; it is only keeping them from facing their fear of relationship.

One of my friends is a powerful leader who is changing the world in a remarkable way. She projects confidence and security when she gets up to speak to an audience or when interacting with other leaders. But when it comes to her relationships with family members and coworkers, she reacts negatively to anything that feels or looks like confrontation, vulnerability, or intimacy. As a result, these relationships are fragile and filled with anxiety. No one experiences the love, intimacy, vulnerability, or truth they need. Like most who wear self-protective armor, this woman doesn't have healthy boundaries (though that's what she might call them); she has walls.

Powerless Relational Dynamics

The classic relational dynamic created by powerless people is called *triangulation.* When you believe that other people are scary, unsafe, and more powerful than you, and when you believe that you need to get them to meet your needs, then you have three possible roles you get to play in relationships: the victim, the bad guy, or the rescuer. If you're the victim, you're looking for a rescuer to make you feel safe and happy. If you're the bad guy, you are using control and intimidation to protect yourself or get someone to meet your needs. If you're a rescuer, you're taking responsibility for someone else's life in an attempt to feel powerful. Powerless people will switch in and out of these roles in relational interactions.

Firstborn children are prime candidates for the rescuer role, because they are often trained from the time they are little to take care of people who are less powerful. Their parents say, "Help Mommy, would you? Go get Junior; he fell down again. I know he made that mess. Just pick it up for me, please, honey. You guys go to the park together, and make sure he doesn't get in trouble." Rescuing people from themselves and taking responsibility for their lives is a familiar role, and *feels* like love. But it actually can create unhealthy codependence.

The subconscious fears driving the triangulation dynamic in victims, bad guys, and rescuers go something like this: *I live in a perpetual state of anxiety because I feel out of control. In adding you to my life, I have increased my anxiety because I can't control you either. I'm threatened by everything you do that I didn't decide for you. Until you let me control you, I don't feel safe in this relationship. Unless you let me control you, you don't love me.*

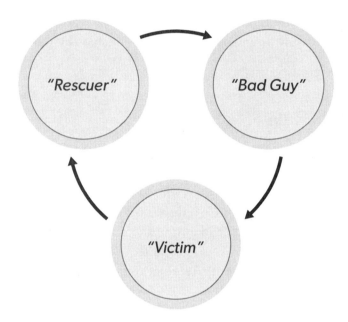

In order to stay in relationship, powerless people make an agreement to exercise mutual control over each other. The unspoken pact between them is, "It's my job to make you happy, and your job to make me happy. And the best way to get you to work on my life is to act miserable. The more miserable I am, the more you will have to try to make me feel better." Powerless people use various tactics, such as getting upset, withdrawing, nagging, ridiculing, pouting, crying, or getting angry, to pressure, manipulate, and punish one another into keeping this pact. However, this ongoing power play does nothing to make them happy and mitigate their anxiety in the long term. In fact, their anxiety only escalates by continually affirming that they are not actually powerful. Any sense of love and safety they feel by gaining or surrendering control is tenuous and fleeting.

A relational bond built on mutual control simply cannot produce anything remotely like safety, love, or trust. It can only produce more fear, pain, distrust, punishment, and misery. And when taken to an extreme, it produces things like domestic violence.

I saw this frightening dynamic firsthand for six years when I taught programs for men and women convicted of domestic violence. The fear those people brought into the room was intense. Some of them had been in relationships for twenty-five years with unending cycles of abuse. One man I worked with had been arrested because he had hit his wife. It was a serious offense. But before that incident, she had knocked him unconscious on two occasions—once with a frying pan and once with a gun. So when she came at him the third time, he took the first punch and knocked her down. The cops took him away because she had a black eye when they showed up and he didn't.

That's the kind of relationship they'd shared for over two decades. They called it love. But it was really two powerless people who had agreed to engage in a lifelong battle for control.

Powerful People

If you heard someone described as a powerful person, you might assume he or she would be the loudest person in the room, the one telling everyone else what to do. But powerful does not mean dominating. In fact, a controlling, dominating person is the very opposite of a powerful person.

Powerful people do not try to control other people. They know it doesn't work, and that it's not their job. *Their job is to control themselves.*

As a result, they are able to consciously and deliberately create the environment in which they want to live. They don't try to get people to respect them; they create a respectful environment by showing respect. They deliberately set the standard for how they expect to be treated by the way they treat others. As they consistently act in responsible, respectful, and loving ways, it becomes clear that the only people who can get close to them are those who know how to show respect, be responsible, and love well.

Life does not happen to powerful people. Powerful people are happening—they are *happening* all the time. They are like a hose that is on full blast in the middle of a mud puddle. The mud does not go up into the hose and contaminate it. Powerful people are not affected or infected by their environment. *They refuse to be victims of others.*

Powerful people also require others to be powerful around them. When they encounter a powerless person, they are not tempted to dive into an unhealthy triangulation dynamic. They hear a victim's sob story and ask, "So what are you going to do about that? What have you tried? What else could you try?" These questions confront powerless people with their responsibility and their capacity to make choices and control themselves. This is the only option a powerful person will offer to powerless people: become powerful, make choices, and control yourself. After failing to get a powerful person to offer them any more options, powerless people will either change in order to start living powerfully or they will find someone else to dump on.

> Powerful people do not try to control other people.

Because they cannot take responsibility for their decisions, powerless people are relegated to reacting to whatever is going on around them on a daily basis. But as a powerful person, I do not simply react to whatever is happening today. I am able to take responsibility for my decisions and the consequences of those decisions—even for my mistakes and failures. I can *respond* to today and *create* my tomorrows. When I leave the house and my wife Sheri tells me to have a good day, I don't say, "I hope my day is good. I hope people are nice to me today. I hope only respectful people have conversations with me today." No, my response is, "I will. I am going to have a good day." I am going to have a good day because I am a powerful person. I have a vision and a mission for my life, and I use the events of each day, whether positive or negative, to direct myself toward them.

Popular opinion or the pressure of others does not sway the language of powerful people. They know exactly what they want and how to communicate their desires. A powerful person says, "I will. I do. I am." Powerful people can say both "Yes" and "No," and mean it. Others can try to manipulate, charm, and threaten, but their answer will stand.

A powerful person's choice to love will stand, *no matter what the other person does or says*. When powerful people say, "I love you," there's nothing that can stop them. Their love is not dependent on being loved in return. It is dependent on their powerful ability to say, "Yes" and carry out that decision. This protects their love from external forces, or from being managed by other people.

Powerful people can *be who they say they are* on a consistent basis. And because they know how to be themselves, they invite those around them to be themselves. Only powerful people can create a safe place to know and be known intimately. They say, "I can be me around you and you can be you around me. We don't need to control each other, and we don't want to control each other. We can have a mutual agreement of respect and honor in which we both work to protect our connection. We stay tied together by the strength of the love we have built, not by the illusion that I can control you or that you need a rescuer."

Becoming Powerful

I've had so many people sit in my office and admit, "I knew before we got married that we shouldn't have done this." These are people who have a relationship with Jesus, are successful in business and other areas of life, and yes, they have a brain that works. Yet when it comes to their relationships, they tell me, "I'm a powerless victim. I want out of the situation that somebody else created for me."

And I have to tell them the bad news: *Everywhere you go, there you are again.*

They will continue to recreate their victimized reality as long as they refuse to repent from it and pursue being powerful.

Repentance means to change the way you think. In order to repent from a life of powerlessness, you will need to identify the lies you believe and the influence those lies have in your life. Once you identify these lies, renounce them and break your agreement with them. Then ask the Holy Spirit to come and tell you the truth. A model repentance prayer could look something like this:

In the name of Jesus, I renounce the lie that [....]

I nail it to the cross of Jesus Christ and send it away from me, never to return again. Holy Spirit, what truth would you like to give me in its place? *(Write down what He tells you.)*

Repeat this prayer for each individual lie that comes up.

Often lies become deeply rooted in a person's core, requiring consistent work to dig them out and replace them with the truth. If you grew up in an abusive, powerless environment, you are probably going to need someone who can help you identify and renounce those lies. If you have access to inner healing tools and ministry like Sozo, I highly recommend that you use them. [2]

No matter what, know that every step on the journey to getting free and being a powerful person is *worth it*. Choosing to say "Yes!" to a life of responsibility and wholeness will be one filled with adventure and joy. Do not let powerlessness and a victim mentality steal from you any longer. You *are* a powerful person who *can* make powerful decisions. And more importantly, you are a powerful person who can choose to love— because He chose to love you. Choosing to love is the most powerful choice you could ever make, and is more rewarding than you could ever imagine.

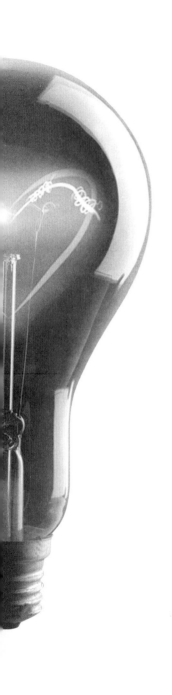

Chapter Two

TURN YOUR LOVE ON

Dave and Anne sat on the couch in my office. "Danny, we need you to help us fix our son." After attending one of my parenting classes, the couple had booked an appointment with me and were desperately hoping I might help them to rein in their boy. The young teenager was extremely out of control and causing more chaos than this family could handle. Dave and Anne took turns describing their son's increasingly destructive escapades, which included smoking pot, running away, breaking windows and furniture, and most recently, taking a joyride in their car. It was obvious that they felt hurt, scared, and increasingly powerless over their situation.

But something else was also going on. I couldn't help but notice that this man and woman were not looking at each other at all. When Dave spoke, Anne looked at the floor, and vice versa. They were clearly disconnected, and I quickly became convinced that *this* disconnected relationship—the one between Dave and Anne—was the real problem in this family.

After they finished their discouraging saga, they looked up, waiting for me to say something.

"Let me ask you a question," I said, aware that changing the subject would be unexpected. "What is the goal of your marriage?"

Sure enough, Dave and Anne looked surprised that I was asking about them and not their son. Then, as they considered my question, their expressions began to follow the classic progression I witness in so many disconnected couples. At first, they looked as though they intended to answer the question easily. But as they realized they didn't have an answer, they grew concerned and then a little distressed.

I knew the thoughts that were running through their minds: *The goal of my marriage? Have I ever even thought about that? What does that mean?* Finally, Anne asked for clarification. "The goal of our marriage—do you mean, like, raising our kids? Sending them to college? Our retirement goals? What do you mean?"

I gave them a sympathetic smile. Then, I looked straight at them, "I'm not interested in the goal of your retirement, parenting, or finances…I'm asking you, what is the goal of your *marriage?*"

A prolonged and uncomfortable silence filled the room.

Finally, Dave offered, "Peace. It would be nice to have some peace in our marriage."

"Peace," I responded, thankful for a start. "Okay."

Then I turned to Anne. "How about you?"

"Well," she muttered, "It would be nice to be able to have a conversation once in a while."

"Peace and conversation," I echoed. "These are your goals for your marriage. Okay."

I paused for effect before asking my next question: "Would I find either or both of those goals in your wedding vows fifteen years ago?"

"No," they both admitted, eyes growing wider.

"Right. So what would you say is the goal of your marriage *right* now?"

That awkward silence filled the room again. Neither could answer the question. They didn't know what their current goal was. They didn't know why, how, or when they had become derailed from the goals they had set out with when they first vowed to love each other, "till death do us part." And what's worse, they were not conscious of their disconnection.

I leaned in closer to them and said, "Many people have this same problem. They are completely unaware of the goal in their relationship. The truth is that every relationship has one of two goals: *connection or disconnection.* These goals are revealed by the skill sets people adopt to achieve them."

"The current goal in this marriage is distance," I continued. "You have developed skill sets around disconnection—around creating a safe distance from one another. Each moment of each day, you are measuring how much distance you need to feel safe around each other. Sometimes the necessary distance is small, and other times it's great. But the current goal is a safe distance, not a safe connection."

Dave and Anne nodded their heads in agreement, but neither broke the silence.

I let them ponder this diagnosis for a moment, and then I asked them the next important question. "Is this the goal you want to keep, or is there another goal that you would want to pursue? If you decide to keep distance as your primary goal, then we are done here. You do not need my help creating distance. You have wonderful distance already without my assistance. I can only help you if you decide you want to pursue a different goal."

Now, here's a moment where some couples get offended at where this confrontation has gone and try to backtrack. "Wait a minute! We're not here to talk about *us*. We're here to talk about our son! *We* are not the problem. How did we even get on this topic…?"

When this happens, I don't protest. I repeat the offer I've laid on the table, and offer some clarification if necessary. "I'm asking you to consider the fact that your son is acting out because he is disconnected from you. I believe this disconnection is a symptom of the fact that you two are not connected to one another. That is the problem I am willing to help you with, if you want my help."

Thankfully in this case, I could tell that Dave and Anne saw the problem and were considering the choice. My priority was to help them realize they were equally responsible to take ownership of the goal for their relationship. Like most disconnected couples, they had arrived at this point by shifting responsibility for the quality of their connection on to one another. If they wanted to commit to the goal of connection and start building a healthy relationship, then they both needed to repent for their powerless mindsets and hold themselves accountable for their own goals in the relationship.

I asked a few more questions to probe a little deeper into what both of them really wanted to experience in their marriage, which was obviously more than peace and conversation. Together, we eventually exposed their mutual secret—the secret commonly hiding in disconnected marriages.

Both wanted to be friends with each other.

They wanted to laugh together, to feel safe, connected, loved, and appreciated. They agreed, "We want a loving, intimate connection with each other. This is the goal we want to have for our marriage."

"Now that's something I want to help you both accomplish!" I exclaimed. "I think you are going to need some help reaching that goal. You've taken the first step—agreeing to pursue a loving, intimate connection. Now we can move on to the next step, which is exchanging the skills and habits that served your old goal of disconnection for skills and habits that will lead you toward connection."

It was time to start digging. "May I ask you a few more questions?"

They both nodded. They had obviously accepted the fact that this meeting had become an intervention for their marriage rather than their son.

"Dave, do you love this woman?"

He paused…and paused. Finally, he murmured, "Mmhmm." He nodded while his mouth attempted to form the word, "Yes."

"Is that a 'yes'?" I asked him, after waiting for nearly a minute.

Dave was facing an uncomfortable truth. The protective skill set he had adopted to pursue his former goal of distance had trained him to avoid offerings of vulnerability—such as telling his wife, "I love you." Would he change right here in front of this woman? Would he let her know that his goal had actually changed to a loving, intimate connection? They had not been vulnerable for such a long time, and now Dave was being forced to take responsibility for himself in his marriage. He couldn't blame Anne for his response. He really did love her, but he was so afraid of being rejected that he was paralyzed.

After another moment, Dave pushed through his fear and stated firmly, "Yes. That is a 'yes'."

"Thank you for that," I replied, acknowledging his courage in making this declaration.

I then turned to Anne with the same question: "Do you love this man?"

She looked at me like a wounded animal. Her eyes reached out to me as though she was looking for a place to hide. She was just as afraid as Dave had been to offer a vulnerable heart. Finally, she took a breath.

"By faith I do," she said.

I couldn't help grinning in stunned amusement. "By faith you do?" I shot back.

Then I asked her again if she loved her husband. I understood that she was scared and had not expected to make this vulnerable choice when they had scheduled their appointment with me. Nonetheless, that was now why they were there.

"Yes," she squeaked.

"Thank you," I said. Turning back to Dave, I asked, "Do you think your wife knows that you love her? Do you think she *feels* your love for her?"

"No," he admitted sheepishly. "I don't think she feels it."

"So you love her, but she doesn't know it," I affirmed. "Your love for her is a secret—a secret you've had to keep in order to pursue your old goal of distance. Is that a secret you want to keep?"

"No," he said immediately. "It sounds pretty silly when you say it like that."

"I'm not trying to judge anything going on between you two," I assured him. "I just want to help you see what is really happening, and then allow you to make informed decisions. I can see that you are not where you want to be in this marriage. But, I know that with the right goals, you will be able to create the connection and relational environment you want."

> "Do you know how your wife feels your love for her?"

I moved on to my next question. "Do you know *how* your wife feels your love for her?"

He slowly looked up at her, then back at me. "I used to think I knew, but I really don't know how she would feel loved by me anymore. With so many failed attempts, I think I've given up."

"Excellent!" I exclaimed. "That is something I wanted to help you realize and understand. Trying again and again to send the message of love without receiving a positive result will leave anyone feeling hurt, powerless, and hopeless. You want to be connected to your wife, but because you cannot seem to repair your 'disconnect,' you have come to believe that she doesn't want a connection with you. This feeling of rejection is painful enough to make you want to change your goal from connecting with her to protecting yourself from her. Does this sound accurate?"

"Totally!" he said, his relief palpable. "That sounds exactly like what has happened in my mind and my heart."

I turned to Anne and asked her if my explanation made sense to her as well. She nodded and confessed that she recognized the same progression of frustration, fear, pain, and withdrawal on her side.

"Are you familiar with *The 5 Love Languages* by Gary Chapman?" I asked them.

"Yes," Dave replied. "I think we read that book several years ago in a study that our home group was doing."

"Great!" I said. "What are Anne's top two love languages?"

He froze. "Uh, well, uh…I don't remember."

He looked like he had just missed the "How Well Do You Know Your Wife for $400" Jeopardy question.

"Okay." We were going to have to go back to square one. "Let me run you through a little refresher course," I said. "We are going to reestablish the route to getting your 'love' turned back on toward one another."

For the next half hour, I reviewed the content of Gary Chapman's book, *The 5 Love Languages* with Dave and Anne. *The 5 Love Languages* provides a set of invaluable tools for building connection between two people—not just in marriage, but also in any close relationship. I recommend that you read Chapman's book if you have not done so. But for the sake of this book, I'm going to provide you with the paraphrased explanations and descriptions of the book's concepts that I usually offer when I teach relationship classes and work with couples.

The 5 Love Languages

Chapman describes five categories of behavior we use to send and receive the message of love. Understanding these categories helps us to identify exactly how we are creating experiences that either promote or discourage feelings of connection. It's important to realize that we are always sending and receiving messages in relationships. We are always moving toward one another or away from one another. The more aware we are of *how* we are doing this, the more we can take responsibility for the messages we are sending and actively build the connections we want.

The five love languages are Touch, Gifts, Quality Time, Acts of Service, and Words of Affirmation. I like to compare these languages to different types of fuel. Every person usually has one primary way that he or she receives and shows love—one type of fuel that fills up his or her "love tank." Knowing someone's love language is as important as knowing what kind of gasoline goes in your car. If you fill a car that takes unleaded gas with diesel fuel, or fill a diesel engine with jet fuel, then it won't be too long before the car breaks down and leaves you stranded on the side of the road. It's just as essential to fill people's love tanks with the language they need in order to function and feel connected in a relationship.

Touch

People who receive "I love you" messages and develop connection through touch need physical contact that others may not necessarily need. Touch people have a "touch meter" planted inside their chests, which connects to every other place in their body like a nerve ending. This meter is counting the nanoseconds since they were last touched. As the meter is depleted by a lack of touch, it registers higher and higher numbers of need. After these numbers reach a certain point, a Touch person begins to feel anxiety increase, and eventually can become easily agitated or aggravated—just like people who get grumpy when they need to eat.

When Touch people are getting the touch they need, they feel safe, nurtured, and loved, and you will see them at their best. Starve this need for affection, either accidently or intentionally, and you'll get the worst person they can be. No matter how they express their anxiety, whether passive or aggressive, you will definitely see the changes in the way they relate to those around them. They will seem "disconnected," even if fifty people are nearby, because they will *feel* alone.

Now, to be clear, the kind of touch that will fill a Touch person's love tank must be healthy, respectful, and offered as a free gift of affection. Unhealthy touch or abuse will not work. Neither will touch offered begrudgingly or out of the fear of unhealthy touch. As a case in point, take the Christian "side hug." The side hug usually says, "I'm attempting to show connection, but I am really afraid of it." If you want to love a Touch person, you will need to overcome any fear of touch and learn ways to express healthy affection.

A Touch person needs to learn how to be powerful in communicating his or her need for touch. Touch is the love language most intrusive to people's personal space, so those who do not require or even like touch often feel uncomfortable meeting this need in others. If a Touch person can communicate his or her needs clearly, without succumbing to anxiety, then both parties can move toward one another effectively.

Acts of Service

Acts of Service folks also have a meter inside them. It marks the ebb and flow of investments into their love bank through the currency of intentional acts of kindness. Each and every time Acts of Service people enter their home or work environment, the meter begins to run. This meter is connected to a video camera in their heads that scans their surroundings and fills or depletes the meter based on what they see has been done, or not done, for them. For example, when they come in the house and see shoes, backpacks, dishes, jackets, and other random items strewn all over the floor, see that the dog needs to be fed, see that the TV is on and no one is watching it, or see anything that needs to be "fixed" or "done," their anxiety begins to climb. This anxiety is even more heightened if they know that they are the only person living in their house who needs that level of order and structure. If that is the case, then the Acts of Service person sees that every mess is his or her problem to solve—all the time. The "kiss-of-death" happens for the Acts of Service person when these important tasks remain chronically undone.

If you have ever been around an anxiety-filled Acts of Service person who has just encountered a messy environment, then you probably know that his or her initial response is often a call for help. Unfortunately, many Acts of Service people have not learned to overcome their anxiety by communicating effectively. They just start barking out phrases like: "Dishes!" "Dog fed!" "Whose backpack?" and "TV is on!" Those in the vicinity either ignore these signals, or, if they feel sufficiently threatened or provoked, start to get up and respond. "That's my backpack." "I will get the trash." "I will feed the dog." These responses help the Acts of Service person's anxiety meter to diminish. However, they do not necessarily fill his or her love tank, because the people in the household did not hear a person asking for love, they heard an upset control freak requiring a bunch of slaves to get their lazy behinds moving. The way to fill an Acts of Service person's love tank is to find out what he or she needs and do it as a free act of love, not coercion.

On their end, Acts of Service people need to learn how to communicate their need and not simply broadcast their anxiety. They need to say, "I feel loved when you take care of things that are important to me. When you don't, you send the message that I am not important to you." After my wife Sheri began communicating this need to me, I became much more proactive in taking care of things she cared about, from chores around the house to putting gas in her car. It was wonderful to discover how doing the simplest tasks made her feel loved and strengthened our connection.

Gifts

Gifts people are constantly soaking up evidence that the people in their life know them and think about them even when they are not around. This evidence lies in a physical token of love. The Gifts person hears, feels, and experiences love through the offering of a gift that says, "I know you. I have been paying attention to you. I have become a student of you, and this gift is a demonstration that I *get* you."

If you're in a relationship with a Gifts person, he or she will probably speak in the language of gifts to you. Gifts people will bring you gifts on a regular basis, particularly if there is a special moment to commemorate the relationship. Anniversaries, birthdays, holidays, and just about any other occasion provide them with endless reasons for gifts. You can bet that they have paid attention to what you like to do, what you like to eat, what you collect, or where you've been in the world. Their gifts to you will symbolize this attention to the details of your life, and they will expect you to reciprocate in kind. Though he or she may never ask the question directly, the Gifts person is wondering, "Now, where is your gift to me?"

The good news is that the gift says far more than a price tag. Whoever coined the phrase, "It's the thought that counts," was definitely a Gifts person. The thought behind the gift is valued far more than the cost, because that's what makes the gift a symbol of devotion. Whatever that thought is, it is answering the driving question of the Gifts person's heart: "Do you know me?" and "Am I on your mind?" A lot of problems ensue when you forget to bring a gift for a special occasion or you give them something without much thought. This sends the message, "No, I'm not thinking about you. I don't pay attention to you." That is not the message you want to send to a Gifts person. Do the work required to find a gift that says, "You were on my mind. I thought you'd like this."

Quality Time

Quality Time people feel love and connection when you find them interesting—with the evidence of this interest being that you want to spend time with them. When a Quality Time person invites you to have a conversation or to join him or her in an activity or hobby, this is an opportunity for you to send the message, "I am interested in you." It may be joining them for a stroll in the garden, letting them show you something they've been reading, or conversing about how your day went.

Sheri's primary love language is Quality Time. My evenings are regularly spent conversing with Sheri about her day. It's an anxiety-reducing and bonding activity. As she processes her day with me, Sheri feels known and cared about because I am interested in what she has to say. My daughter Brittney is also a Quality Time person. When I am with either my wife or daughter, I have made it a habit to turn my whole focus and attention to what they are sharing with me because this makes them feel loved.

For Quality Time people, pain enters the relationship when you don't listen or pay attention to them. When you don't make time to fully engage with them, you send the the ugly message that you are not interested in them, or worse, that they are not important to you. Quality time is not necessarily quantity time; the level of genuine interest and engagement you give determines quality. Engage in the activity or conversation with all your energy and attention, and engage with them on the deepest level.

Words of Affirmation

Words of Affirmation people feel most enjoyed and appreciated when your words and body language include a positive tone of voice, facial expressions, and word choice. They notice the "spirit" or intent of the words exchanged, and that aspect impacts them powerfully. For the Words of Affirmation person, anxiety rises and falls with the way words are used in conversation. A simple word of encouragement goes a long way toward creating safety and connection. Love flows into them with every positive word, and they relax as they experience someone verbally expressing their enjoyment in them.

Conversely, when the tone of a conversation or interaction turns negative or critical, the anxiety level of the Words of Affirmation person begins to climb. Hurt is caused primarily through critical, negative, or angry words. These make them feel that they have no other choice but to defend themselves from such a painful experience. Some withdraw into themselves, while others come out swinging with their own arsenal of sarcasm and negativity.

How do you give correction or constructive criticism to a Words of Affirmation person? You use the "hero sandwich." These sandwiches have twice as much "I love you" as they do criticism. The bread is the nice, positive, reinforcing words of affirmation that communicate your love, and the meat is the constructive criticism. It sounds something like this: "I need to tell you something. But first I want you to know that I love you very much and you are extremely important to me. That thing you are doing is driving me nuts, and I need you to stop it. Even though this is happening, I want you to remember that I love you with all my heart."

The "hero sandwich" keeps the Words of Affirmation person in the conversation by filling his or her love tank with affirmation. The two "I love you" messages drive down the anxiety and create safety, even though you are communicating that you are upset. This approach allows honest, open relationships to form with someone who might otherwise shut down in the face of critical feedback.

What Is Your Goal?

After reviewing the love languages with Dave and Anne, I asked Dave what he thought Anne's primary love languages were.

"I'd say she's Words of Affirmation and Gifts," he said, looking in her direction, hoping for some affirming words himself.

Anne nodded and said, "I think I'm Quality Time in there somewhere too, but yes, those sound good. I would really like to develop those things in our relationship."

"All right, that's good news!" I encouraged them. "That is some good information right there. Knowing where the target is makes this a much more enjoyable game, don't you think? No more golfing in the dark for you! Now you can see what you are aiming for."

"Yeah, that's true," Dave agreed.

"With this knowledge of what love feels like to your wife, how would you say you are doing in offering her Words of Affirmation and Gifts to communicate your love?"

"Not very well at all," he said. "I can do better. But I know this is going to help me a lot. I feel like I have some power now in this relationship and in our family again."

Both Dave and Anne were smiling at this point. Then I asked Anne the same question about Dave's love languages. She said his were Touch and Words of Affirmation. She also agreed that she saw room for improvement in speaking Dave's love languages.

> *"I love you" messages drive down the anxiety and create safety.*

The last thing I did with Dave and Anne that day was to give them some tools about how they could communicate and keep their love flowing while they worked out misunderstandings and conflicts—tools you'll be reading about in future chapters. They left my office with the clear understanding that they simply had to learn how to reduce the disconnection and increase the connection between them before the atmosphere of their home and their relationship with their son would ever improve. They grasped the importance of keeping love turned on full blast in order to chase away the destructive forces of fear and anxiety.

It's Your Turn

Now, I have a few questions for you. What is the goal in your close relationships? Are you trying to create a safe connection or a safe distance? Are you building a skill set to move away from or control the distance between you and your husband, wife, friend, child, etc.? Or are you building a skill set to move toward them and keep your love on no matter what?

Until you commit to the goal of connection, all the relational tools in the world are not going to help you. It's only when you decide to take responsibility to pursue connection that you will discover just why you need these tools. It's only when you commit to moving toward someone that you will seek the knowledge and skills necessary to reach them.

The choice to pursue the goal of connection will bring you right up against the real conflict that lies at the core of every relationship. It is a spiritual battle—a heart battle—drawn between the two most powerful forces that drive us: *fear and love*. If you want to be a powerful person capable of building intimate relationships, then it is absolutely vital that you learn how these forces operate and align yourself with love.

Chapter Three

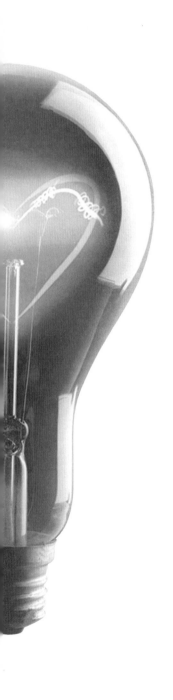

THE BATTLE BETWEEN FEAR AND LOVE

How is it that two people who vowed to love and care for one another for a lifetime, as Dave and Anne did, end up slowly moving away from one another, until the goal and practices of disconnection become entrenched in their relationship? Do people just decide one day to stop loving one another?

The answer, sadly, is *yes*. But it's usually not a conscious decision. Most often it is a reaction to pain or the fear of pain.

Pain teaches us to react from the moment we enter the earth. The first reaction we have to pain is to cry. As newborns, when someone bigger responds to our cries by doing something to make us feel better, we learn that crying is a helpful reaction to pain or discomfort.

As we grow up, our reactions teach us how to avoid pain. As a child, even though my mother told me not to touch a hot stove, I had to satisfy my own curiosity. *"Hot" is bad?* Then I experienced the blistering effects of a second-degree burn and learned that "hot" was indeed "bad." After that, my behavior around hot stoves was instinctively driven by the goal of pain avoidance.

Human beings generally develop three classic reactions to the threat of pain—fight, flight, or freeze. All of these reactions have the same goal: *distance!* We want to get away from scary things that can hurt us. Take rattlesnakes for instance. While few of us have ever been bitten by a rattler, we all know what would happen if we were. Unsurprisingly, very few of us keep pet rattlesnakes in our homes. Those who handle rattlesnakes do so with instruments of control and violence, such as cages, prods, guns, and gloves. No one is looking to create a loving, lasting, intimate relationship with a rattlesnake. It's a basic human instinct—when the threat of harm is high, the level of love is low.

Our relationships with people are a lot more complicated than our relationships with rattlesnakes, because other people offer us both comfort and protection from pain as well as the threat of pain. The mom who fed you and changed your diaper in response to your cries is also the one who yelled at you and slapped your hand away from a hot stove. The dad who taught you to ride a bike is also the one who could never tell you, "I love you." And the wife or husband who promised you unconditional love is the person who could break your heart with rejection and betrayal.

The question at stake is *how* you will react to the pain you experience in relationships. If you fall back on the classic fear-driven reactions, you will necessarily start treating people like rattlesnakes. You will either run away or try to control people so they won't hurt you. The problem is that neither of these options will help you pursue and protect the goal of connection in a relationship.

Unfortunately, many people grow up in relational cultures that used "rattlesnake" tools to deal with pain and the fear of pain—tools that control, manipulate, remove freedom, threaten, and withhold love. These are the tools of powerlessness. The message they instill is, "It's my job to control you. If you don't let me control you, then I will introduce pain to teach you that lesson." I'm not talking about parents protecting their children from harm or introducing appropriate consequences for their choices in order to help them learn. I'm talking about parents who believe it is their job to make their child's choices and to punish them when they don't comply with their orders. They may have said, "This is going to hurt me more than it hurts you," but what their children learned was that if they didn't surrender control, the most powerful adult in their life would get mad, threaten, withhold love, or hurt them in some way. They learned that in any given relationship, only one person at a time gets to be powerful. And ultimately, they learned to believe the lie that drives and protects the cycle of fear, control, punishment, and disconnection in relationships—*the lie that we can and should control other people.*

Unless they repent from this lie, they cannot help but bring controlling behaviors into their adult relationships. Plenty of people grow up saying, "I am never going to be like my parents. Never!" Yet, the first time they run into a scary or painful relational situation, they find themselves spouting out the same exact words, making the same faces, and dragging around the same manipulative, fear-inflicting tools that once caused them so much pain. They may have *tried* to learn some new relational tools, but the minute they got scared, their real beliefs were unmasked. In the face of pain, they align themselves with the goals of fear—distance, control, and punishment.

Again, it's important to remember that fear-based reactions to pain are instinctive, which means that they operate at a very different level in your brain than conscious, rational choices. You execute them without thinking. And because they come so naturally, they seem *normal.*

One expression of this natural, fear-based human "normal" is that you tend to surround yourself with people who feel safe. "Safe" people are those who agree with you and reinforce what you already believe about the world. If you were to take a survey of all the people close to you, then you would probably find that they share similar core values, political affiliations, education, and social or economic status. When you get around someone who doesn't support your worldview, it usually triggers your defenses. Whether you know it or not, your brain is saying, "I don't want that person around. They scare me. I want them far away because I want to be comfortable in my beliefs bubble." It's human nature to maintain your comfort zone.

Nevertheless, as natural as it is, this fear-based "normal" is a major problem. Instinctive reactions to pain do not bring out the best in human beings. On a social level, oppression, injustice, racism, war, and most other social evils can be traced back to the instinctive fear of people who are different. On a personal level, fear-based reactions cause most misunderstandings and hurt in relationships.

If you want to preserve relationships, then you must learn to *respond* instead of *react* to fear and pain. Responding does not come naturally. You can react without thinking, but you cannot respond without training your mind to think, your will to choose, and your body to obey. It is precisely this training that brings the best qualities in human beings—like courage, empathy, reason, compassion, justice, and generosity—to the surface. The ability to exercise these qualities and respond gives you other options besides disconnection in the face of relational pain.

Powerful people are not slaves to their instincts. Powerful people can respond with love in the face of pain and fear. This "response-ability" is essential to building healthy relationships.

Created For Freedom

In order to begin training yourself to respond in love, the first thing you need to accept is this truth: *You cannot control other people. The only person you can control—on a good day—is yourself.*

This is a fundamental principle of human freedom. We were designed to be free. How do we know this? God put two trees in the garden. He gave us a choice. Without choice, we don't have freedom, and more importantly, we don't have love, which requires freedom. God chose us, loves us, and wants us to choose Him and love Him in return. So He gave us a free choice, even though it necessarily meant risking our rejection and the devastation of a disconnected relationship. The tragedy of the Fall actually proclaims that He does not want to control us. He didn't control us in the Garden, and He doesn't control us now.

Many people find this difficult to believe. If you were raised with a powerless, fear-driven mindset based on the belief that you can control people and they can control you, then you will naturally perceive God as a controlling punisher. You will take the laws of the Old Testament— all the verses and stories about wrath, judgment, and the fear of the Lord— and conclude, "See, God wants to control us, and we need to be controlled. Our hearts are desperately wicked and we can't be trusted, so God uses the threat of punishment to maintain the distance between us and Him."

The problem is that the Bible doesn't show us a God who is pursuing the goal of distance between Himself and a bunch of scary sinners. Instead, the Bible reveals a God who is relentlessly closing that distance and paying the ultimate price to repair the disconnection we created in our relationship. God's number one goal with us is connection, and nothing— neither pain nor death—will prevent Him from moving toward us and responding to us with love.

> *The only person you can control—on a good day—is yourself.*

His perfect love for us is absolutely *fearless*. He is not afraid of us, and He never will be. His Gospel message is, "I love you no matter what. I am not afraid of your mistakes, and you don't have to be afraid of them either. You don't have to be afraid of other people's mistakes. They may be painful; many things in this life may be painful. But pain and the fear of pain no longer have the power to control you. You are always free to choose. So, what are you going to do? Remember that I am always here for you, whatever you choose."

God is continually moving toward you in love and giving you the choice to love Him. He never takes your choices away. 2 Corinthians 3:17 says, "Where the Spirit of the Lord is, there is liberty." [1] The more God fills your life, the more freedom you will have.

Fear Is Your Enemy

While God is not afraid of sin or sinners, most of us are. We're afraid of people's mistakes, and we're afraid of our own. It's no wonder our entire society, including our court system, is set up in such a way that fear and punishment are the solutions to bad behavior. And as long as we operate out of fear, we will inevitably continue to reproduce distance and disconnection in our relationships with God, others, and ourselves. The cycle can only be broken by repenting from the lie that we can control other people and by accepting the truth that *we must control ourselves.*

As soon as you begin to believe this truth and stop trying to control people, you're going to be confronted with a lot of resistance from the old normal. And it won't give way to Heaven's normal without a fight.

Remember how hard it was for Dave to tell me that he loved his wife? The minute he turned from the goal of distance and disconnection to the goal of connection, he was plunged into a battle against fear. This is because fear and love are enemies. They come from two opposing kingdoms. Fear comes from the devil, who would like nothing more than to keep you permanently disconnected and isolated. Love comes from God, who is always working to heal and restore your connection with Him and other people and bring you into healthy, life-giving relationships.

Fear and love have opposite agendas and opposite strategies for achieving them. They *cannot coexist* in a person, relationship, or culture.

God is very clear that the Spirit He put in you is not the spirit of fear, but the Spirit of love: "You have not been given a spirit of fear, but of power, and of love, and a sound mind." [2] He's also clear that partnering with the Spirit of love is the way to displace fear in your life. John wrote, "There is no fear in love. But perfect love casts out fear, because fear has to do with punishment. The one who fears is not made perfect in love." [3] If you want to partner with the Holy Spirit, then you must have a strict "no tolerance" policy about fear and punishment in your life and relationships. It doesn't matter how long you've used those tools—they have got to go!

Learning to partner with the Spirit of love requires you to become powerful. That is a serious challenge. When Paul told Timothy that the spirit of love is also the spirit of power and a sound mind, he implied that its opposite, the spirit of fear, is the spirit of powerlessness and a weak, divided mind. When you grow up partnering with the spirit of fear, as most of us do, you learn to simply hand over your brain and your power, letting fear take control. But as soon as you decide to partner with the spirit of love, *you have to think and make powerful choices.*

Dave and Anne couldn't even remember making a decision to listen to fear and turn their love off. But in order to turn their love back on, they had to marshal their internal resources to think, decide, and act. They had to become powerful and exercise self-control in order to say, "Yes, I love my spouse."

> "You have not been given a spirit of fear, but of power, and of love, and a sound mind."

The choice Dave and Anne made to turn their love on in my office that day was, in a way, even more powerful than the choice they made to get married in the first place, because they made it *after* experiencing a history of pain with one another. They no longer had illusions about the worst fear and pain could bring out in them. They knew that their choice to love one another could not be conditioned by what the other person did or did not do, and that it had to be strong enough to withstand the fear and pain that derailed them in the past. They understood better than before just how powerful they needed to be to make that choice. And wonderfully, they decided to be powerful, to respond in love and cast out fear in their relationship. They did it—and so can you!

Controlling Ourselves Toward Connection

Do you want to win the battle between fear and love in your relationships? You can start by making these two fundamental commitments:

1   *It's my job to control myself. I do not get to control other people.*

2   *My number-one goal and priority in relationships is building and protecting connection.*

These commitments are among the most powerful choices you can make, and they will require more of you than anything you can imagine. But the person you will become, and the relationships you will be capable of experiencing as a result, are absolutely worth the investment.

After making these commitments, you will need to acquire several skill sets in order to follow through with them. First, as we explored in the last chapter, you need to be able to communicate love consistently in ways that people can hear and receive. This sounds simple, but if you have grown up in a fear-based, love-starved relational culture, it can be revolutionary to break the silence and start actively communicating what has hitherto been one of your best-kept secrets: "I love you. My relationship with you is really important to me."

In a counselling session, it is common to uncover the fact that the individual was raised by a parent who wouldn't or couldn't say, "I love you." Often, this person has spent his entire life blowing off this glaring omission, trying to accept "by faith" that his mother or father really loved him. "Oh, I know my dad loved me. He had a hard time saying it. He never said it to anybody. But I knew. He was my dad. He loved me."

Of course, the person is getting inner healing because Dad's silence allowed anxiety to persist in their relationship and weaken their connection. The pain of this disconnection is why the person is a mess.

If you want to cast out all the fear in your relationships, then you need to leave no room for doubt in people's minds and hearts that you truly love them.

It's amazing how much you can strengthen a relational connection and resolve relational problems by simply speaking in one another's love languages. Each display of love, no matter how seemingly small, is a powerful act of spiritual warfare that removes anxiety from the environment, replaces it with freedom and safety, and invites each person to bring his or her best self forward in the relationship. Never forget that scared people are bound to show you their worst. People who feel loved, on the other hand, will usually show you their best.

As you manage your love toward others and pursue the goal of connection, you will need feedback so you can understand how you're affecting them and identify where you need to make adjustments. You will also need to offer the same kind of feedback to them. This is where the second skill set for building connection comes in—communication. We will explore this skill set more fully in the second section of this book, but for now, I'll say that healthy communication is all about providing people with honest, relevant information about how their behavior is affecting your life. It's not about judging them or telling them how they need to change. It is about trusting them to do whatever they need to do to protect and nourish your connection and letting them know that you will do the same.

God practices healthy communication with you. In Psalm 32:8, David speaks for God thus: "I will instruct you and teach you in the way you should go; I will guide you with My eye." [4] This sounds a little strange at first. How is God going to lead you with His eyeball? He can't control you with His eyeball…and that's the point. What He can do with His eye is show you how He feels about the choices you're making and how they're affecting His heart. The eyes are the windows to the heart. When God shows you how your choices affect His heart and your connection with Him, then you get to choose how you will respond to this information. Will you adjust, if necessary, in order to protect your connection with Him? That is the real test of a healthy relationship.

The third and final skill set you need in order to control yourself and pursue the goal of connection, which we will explore in the final section of the book, is a new plan for dealing with the things that threaten your connections. You need to have a punishment-free, control-free, fear-free plan for dealing with people who make mistakes, engaging in conflict, and setting healthy boundaries.

Your success in this plan is fully determined by how powerful you are willing to become. Will you become a person who can keep your love on, no matter what? A powerful person says, "I am going to be okay no matter what you do. You can hurt me, but you cannot make me turn my love off. I am relentlessly going to do what I have to do to protect my connection with you, no matter what." When you can say and do this in the face of fear, mistakes, and pain, you have already won the battle between fear and love.

Chapter Four

BUILDING HEALTHY RELATIONSHIPS

M y wife Sheri and I are a testimony of the power of choosing to keep love on against all odds. Both my parents were married three times. Sheri's mom and dad were each married three times as well, and her stepfather, who raised her from the time she was two years old, was also married three times.

Between our two sets of parents, there were fifteen marriages. Each one obviously affected our lives as a couple. So, when the time came for Sheri and I to get married, we sought pre-marital counseling from Bill Johnson.

There was no such thing as a pre-marriage class back then. Our "counseling" consisted of two private sessions with Pastor Bill. During the first session, we took a test called the Taylor Johnson Compatibility Assessment. In the second session, we went over the test results. Supposedly everything looked okay, so we decided to get married.

Twelve years later, Sheri and I sat in Bill's living room discussing the opportunity to be associate pastors at Bethel. Somehow the topic of our marriage came up, and Bill scratched his chin. "This reminds me of that note that was on your assessment," he said.

"What note?" I asked.

He looked at me expectantly, "That Taylor Johnson thing we did in your pre-married counseling sessions—remember the note that was on it when it came back?"

Sheri and I both drew blanks. "Um…no."

"I didn't tell you about the note?" he asked, looking confused.

Sheri and I leaned toward him. Both of us were keenly interested to find out whether this "note" would answer years of questions swirling around our marriage. "What note?"

"You didn't tell them?" Beni, Bill's wife, asked in disbelief.

"Tell us what?" Sheri and I prodded.

"Oh, that's weird," Bill said. "I thought I told you about it a while ago. Well, for ten years I gave that assessment to couples and sent them off to a psychologist. He ran them through his computer and then mailed me the results."

"Okay," Sheri nodded, urging him on.

"When I got your test back, it came with a Post-It note on it—the first time in ten years there had ever been a Post-It note." He paused. "The psychologist explained that the test shows the points where two people's lives are supposed to touch in compatibility in order to predict a successful relationship. Well…you two did not touch on any point—you had parallel lines. According to that test, you were completely incompatible."

I felt my eyes bugging out of my head.

Bill kept going, oblivious to our astonishment. "According to the psychologist, between the differences in your personalities and the fifteen marriages that had gone on with your parents, your chances of success were negligible. His Post-It note said something to this effect—'Do whatever you can to stop these two human beings from being in the same house together!'"

It felt like a small bomb had gone off. We stared at each other in shock, trying to absorb the fact that:

a) some psychologist had warned us to not get married, and

b) Bill had not told us.

It was a pretty funny moment, looking back.

Finally, I said, "Well Bill, that helps explain why the first decade of our marriage was hell!"

Our first ten years of marriage were a constant struggle. Sheri and I came up against serious challenges created by our vastly different personalities, broken relational histories, and natural human fears. There were plenty of moments where we could have decided we'd had enough because it just wasn't working. But we both chose to stay invested in our connection and keep trying. We chose to embrace the unique things that made us different and learned what unconditional love and acceptance could produce when two people refused to give up on each other.

Bill must have known deep down not to give us that note. I can tell you now that what Sheri and I have created is a beautiful thing. If that psychologist could only see us now! The connection we have built and the life we enjoy together keeps getting better and better. Our marriage is a miracle in every way.

Thanks to my journey with Sheri, I have more hope than anyone else I know for people who are going through marital problems. If you are blessed to grow up in a healthy relational environment, then it is possible for you to simply inherit good relational tools, never really appreciating just how powerful and costly they are. But when, as Sheri and I did, you have to pay the price to go find these tools after receiving a pile of dangerous, broken tools from your family environment, then you have a different perspective. Acquiring the tools and wisdom to build a healthy connection in our marriage was like discovering the polio vaccine. Learning to make the reversals we have discussed in the previous chapters—from powerless to powerful, from control to self-control, from the goal of distance to the goal of connection, and from fear to love—were nothing short of revolutionary. And we are supremely confident that anyone can make these reversals and build or restore healthy intimate connections in their lives, even after years of disconnection and brokenness.

The Foundation: Unconditional Love and Acceptance

Healthy relationships truly are the most valuable, meaningful, and satisfying of human experiences. But what are the qualities that make up a healthy relational connection? If you don't know, then you won't be able to assess whether or not your relational practices are helping to build and strengthen a connection. Like a house, a relational connection needs to have specific elements to complete its structure, or it will be unsafe and vulnerable to disaster.

As with all houses, building starts with the foundation. The foundation of a healthy relationship is an agreement to practice unconditional acceptance and unconditional love.

Unconditional acceptance says, "You are not me and I am not you. You get to be you and I get to be me in this relationship." This does not mean you have to unconditionally accept one another's behaviors. Rather, it means that you do not control one another.

Not controlling someone while not accepting his or her (negative) behavior looks something like this. Imagine my son has been playing in the backyard and happens to step in doggy-doo. I don't want his shoes to touch my carpet, so I meet him at the back door.

"Son," I say, "Feel free to come in the house once the dog mess is gone. You can take your shoes off or wash your shoes off."

"Dad!?"

"I love you. Take your time." My voice is calm, and I have a smile on my face.

Not wanting dog mess in the house doesn't mean I don't want my son in the house. I separate him from the mess. I can love him and still require him to eliminate the mess before he comes inside. He may try to force his way in. However, I can assure you, people can't force their way into my house—or into my trust, vulnerability, and intimacy. I am the only person who allows people into my house. This is not controlling someone else—this is controlling myself.

Unconditional love says, "No matter what you do, I am going to pursue the goal of connection with you."

Unconditional love says, "No matter what you do, I am going to pursue the goal of connection with you." Anxiety naturally arises when personal differences show up in a relationship, and fear will tempt us to run away from each other. But in committing to unconditional love, we commit to keep moving toward each other even when we're scared. We will do whatever it is we need to do to protect our connection.

Sometimes you have to be willing to agree to disagree over something in order to maintain your connection. My relationship with an old and dear friend was almost destroyed over our different opinions on a certain moral issue. However, we decided to put our relationship first and be at peace even though we approached the issue in opposite ways. We still don't agree, but we won't let our disagreement create a wedge in our connection.

Conditional love and acceptance means that we are willing to pull away from our connection under certain circumstances. The minute we happen to scare the other person or they scare us; we will be tempted to withhold our love and disconnect. And because disconnection only produces more fear and anxiety, we will widen our distance at an alarming rate. This threat effectively prevents two people from feeling free to be themselves because they instinctively know the connection won't be strong enough to handle it.

In contrast, when we commit to unconditional love and acceptance, we protect each other's freedom. Everything that we offer to the relationship comes freely from our hearts, not under coercion. Yes, committing to pursue and protect my connection with you means that I will be thinking about how my decisions will affect you while making adjustments accordingly. But managing myself to protect our connection is the ultimate expression of freedom—that is what it means to be a powerful person.

Without the foundation of unconditional love and acceptance in a relationship, we simply cannot be free to be ourselves. It's only when we remove the option of distance and disconnection from our relationships that we create a safe place to be ourselves. We cast out fear, inviting each other to bring our best selves forward.

Yes, it's vulnerable and scary to keep your love on toward someone who has become a perceived threat—you cannot guarantee what he or she is going to do. But you can guarantee your own choice. And you can *always* choose connection.

Seven Pillars of Healthy Relationships

The foundation of unconditional love and acceptance determines the longevity and resilience of a relational connection. This foundation consistently supports the other elements that make up a healthy relationship—elements I've dubbed the "Seven Pillars."

In Proverbs 9:1 we read, "Wisdom has built her house; she has hewn her seven pillars…" [1] The House of Wisdom represents the Kingdom of God, the domain where God's ultimate reality is expressed in its perfect design. At the center of this Kingdom is the dynamic and perfect relationship of the Trinity, which sets the pattern for all relationships.

The pillars that hold up this house represent the core values of Kingdom life, the core values of healthy relationships. These core values are love, honor, self-control, responsibility, truth, faith, and vision.

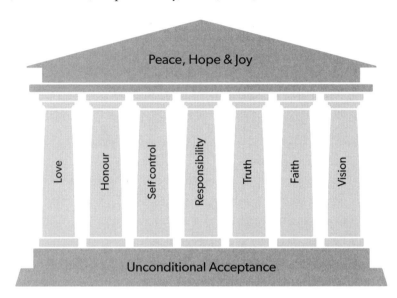

The Pillar of Love

Love is a word of many meanings. We use it to talk about our favorite sports, foods, hobbies, and movies. We also read 1 Corinthians 13:13—"the greatest of these is love" [2] —and acknowledge that love is the biggest, most important, and most powerful thing in the universe.

So, what does love mean in the context of a relationship?

The pillar of love is comprised of a commitment, an action, and a result. The commitment part is this: "I care about you and value you—*all* of you. I care about your soul, spirit, body, relationships, dreams, and destiny." The action part is demonstrating care and value in many ways and in many situations as you get to know a person over time. And the result of these actions is that the person feels loved! They feel safe, valued, connected, nourished, protected, and understood.

I knew a young couple that had one of those classic mother-in-law problems. The husband's mother and his wife had a constant power struggle because the husband had trouble setting boundaries with his mother. Then, right before the wife was about to give birth to their third child, his mother called and asked if she could move in for a while. The husband finally listened to his wife and had a rather difficult but necessary "you can't stay here" conversation with his mother. For one of the first times in their married life, his wife felt safe, protected, and loved during a situation involving his mother.

If your "love" isn't producing things like safety, peace, and trust in your relationship, it probably shouldn't be called love. There are millions of people around the world who call what they have in a relationship "love." Looking closer you find that they are people who cannot fully be themselves because it's not safe—they consistently withhold things and set conditions based on what they will give up to the other person. If you want to test the quality of love in a relationship, then you need to ask one another, "Do you feel safe? Do you feel cared for? Do you feel valued and significant? Do you feel protected? Do you feel pursued and known?"

Remember, perfect love casts out fear. The most immediate sign that the pillar of love is growing strong in your relationship is that all fear is leaving as courage, freedom, and safety are felt and expressed.

The Pillar of Honor

Honor, like submission, is a term that has been misused and abused, particularly in connection with marriage. People see it as something that is expected, rather than something that is given. This is backward. When honor is expected or even demanded, it becomes just another word for handing the control, power, and value over to one person in the relationship. A relationship where one person has all the power is one of dishonor, not honor.

God modeled honor when He transformed us from slaves to friends, from orphans to sons. He stooped low to bring us to His level. He used

His power to make us powerful, insisting that we be equal partners in His plan to bring Heaven to earth. This is the pattern for honor in relationships. True honor is the practice of two powerful people putting one another before themselves, empowering one another, working together to meet one another's needs, and adjusting as necessary in order to move together toward the shared goals of the relationship. Honor is also the practice of calling out the best in one another. This can be expressed both in words of praise—"You are amazing!"—and in words of correction—"Hey, you are way too awesome to be acting like that! Remember who you are and stop it."

I remember when my son, Taylor was struggling to get a job. He was living on his own, had few jobs here and there, but for the most part was unemployed. I found out that he wasn't doing his best to get a job, so I let him know I wasn't going to help him financially anymore.

"Dad!" he complained. "It's just been really hard to find a job."

"Son, you are Taylor Silk," I said. "You can do whatever you want to do. Remember who you are. If you want a job you can get a job."

After he stopped protesting, he thanked me for believing in him, and went out and got a job within a week.

Honor allows us to keep high levels of value for and faith in people, even when they demonstrate how different from us they are (which can be scary) and when they make mistakes (which can also be scary). Typically, people allow differences and mistakes to lower their respect and value for other people. But you know the pillar of honor is strong in a relationship when you can look at the other person and say, "You are really different from me. It makes me sad when I see you making that choice. But I love you. I value you, I believe in you, and I am here for you in this relationship."

The Pillar of Self-Control

Self-control is at the core of being a powerful person. Self-control means that you can tell yourself what to do, and you can make yourself do it. It sounds simple enough, but telling yourself what to do and obeying yourself can be quite an accomplishment! For most of us, it's a good day when we obey ourselves.

In order for us to practice self-control, we must have a goal. We must have something we are saying "yes" to, which necessarily comes with things that we must say "no" to. We use self-control to maneuver ourselves toward this "yes." This goal must be entirely our own. The minute another person is choosing and managing our goals for us, we have left self-control behind.

When I practice self-control in a relationship, I take full responsibility for managing my love and pursuing my goal of connection. If I ever turn my love off toward you, it is 100% my fault, no matter what you may have done. Self-control removes the option of blaming others for our choices.

When two people show one another that they are able to control themselves on a consistent basis, they demonstrate that they are reliable and trustworthy. You can tell that the pillar of self-control is strong in a relationship when you don't have to spend time wondering whether or not the other person will follow through with something he or she promised to do.

Self-control is at the core of being a powerful person.

Conversely, a lack of self-control creates anxiety in a relationship because you cannot trust one another to manage yourselves toward your goals. For example, say a young man gets a great job, his dream job. The job involves a lot of unsupervised time, but his boss trusts him to manage his time and work without needing to hover over him. Around the time he gets this job, this young man gets a girlfriend. As time progresses, he allows Ms. Girlfriend to take up more and more time, and puts his awesome job on the back burner. Work piles up, stressing him, his boss, and everyone else who depends on him doing what he said he would do. The end result is a jeopardized job and a jeopardized relationship with his boss.

We must learn how to manage our freedom. When we find ourselves with more freedom than self-control, then that freedom erodes the quality of our life and friendships. Self-control is what allows us to manage increasing levels of freedom in our life and relationships.

The Pillar of Responsibility

When we break the word "responsibility" down, we find that it literally means "ability to respond." If you remember, a response is the opposite of a reaction. "Response-ability" is the capacity to face any situation and make powerful choices that are consistent with who you say you are. It is a refusal to run away from difficulties or any part of your life or reality that you happen to dislike. When you take full ownership of your life in this way, you gain confidence and momentum in making good decisions.

Say you decide to spend a day driving around New York City. You pick up your rental car at JFK and follow the signs to Manhattan. You know you want to get from the Brooklyn Bridge to Central Park, but you don't have a map. At each intersection you crane your neck to read the street signs, senses on high alert in the swirl of honking taxis and pedestrians. Every hundred feet or so, you must make another decision about where to go, which becomes more and more difficult as you realize you have no idea where you are. Pretty soon, your anxiety levels are spiking into crisis territory because you are having such a difficult time responding to your environment.

But what if you head to New York with a GPS that tells you, "Turn left in 300 feet, drive three miles, and arrive at destination on left"? Your anxiety stays low because you trust that your GPS is going to lead you down the right path. If you make a mistake, you can count on it to show you a different route. You are able to respond to your circumstances and get where you want to go.

When the pillar of responsibility is strong in a relationship, it's like having a GPS. You are both confident and relaxed because you have a plan, an inner compass, that can be relied on to help you to respond with love and powerful choices *in any circumstance.* This plan grows out of your core commitments to control yourself, cast out fear with love, and pursue the goal of connection. It's very powerful when two people can look at one another and know that no matter what happens, each of you knows what you are going to choose to do.

Banning Liebscher, founder of Jesus Culture, is great example of a man with a plan, vision, and mission for his life. Let's just say he has one powerful internal GPS. Throughout the course of his life, he has had many opportunities to compromise or divert his life and energy away from his calling. But he has such an intense focus and personal responsibility for his mission that he has experienced enormous success at a young age. Furthermore, he has not been overwhelmed or distracted due to his ability to respond to his abundance in the right way. He has weathered many storms and strengthened his covenant relationships because of his commitment to God's purposes in the unfolding of his intentional life. That is what a life looks like when the pillar of responsibility is strong!

The Pillar of Truth

When I ask people to write down a list of qualities they want in their relationships, I almost always see trust or trustworthiness somewhere close to the top. However, for many people, trust means, "I need to be able to anticipate your decisions. I need to know that you would do what I would do." On one level, that's absolutely right—two people in a relationship need to be on the same page about who they are and what they are going after. But if trust hinges on my ability to anticipate your behavior, then our connection is going to be threatened. Every time you do something that I would never do, I begin to think: *I didn't anticipate that! You aren't acting like me. I would never do that to you. Did you really just bring that into our relationship? How could you do that? I can't trust you now!* This version of trust quickly turns to mistrust, which is just another word for fear—the enemy of love and connection.

Incidentally, many people get disillusioned and hurt when God does not do what they think He should have done. Because they could not predict His behavior, they decide not to trust Him. Does that mean God's not trustworthy? Absolutely not. If the Perfect One is not trustworthy, then how can imperfect people ever be trustworthy? We have to be able to trust people even when they do things we wouldn't do or we will end up very isolated.

Two people who walk through life together are always going to be getting to know one another on some level. Life is not static or contained. There will always be mystery, unexpected circumstances to face, and fresh seasons of growth. So we need a pillar in our relationships that makes room for this—the pillar of truth. The pillar of truth sustains trust in a relationship.

> I display trust by telling you the truth.

Like all the other pillars, truth is built through powerful choices, choices that are all about what you are going to do, not about what the other person is going to do. I don't demand your trust; I *display trust* by telling you the truth. I crack open my chest and show you what is going on inside of me. I choose to show you what I am experiencing in my relationship with you, no matter what. Each time I do that, I leave you with good information, and you get to make better decisions because you can now see *me*. Practicing truth is a very vulnerable thing to do, but is absolutely necessary when building any relationship worth keeping.

When we allow patterns of mistrust and hiding ourselves to develop in our relationships, we end up having conversations like this:

"What's wrong?"

"Nothing. Like you care."

"What? I do care. Tell me what's going on. What is the problem?"

"You want to know the problem? You are the problem. You just walk by me and don't even say 'hi.' All day long, every time I see you, nothing!"

And you say you care. You don't care about anybody but yourself."

We call this an exchange of truth, but actually I have told you nothing about me—I have only told you four things that are wrong with you. I'm not really being vulnerable and showing you my heart; I'm judging you. A conversation where truth is being exchanged would sound a little different:

"What's wrong?"

"Well, basically I got hurt. I am feeling hurt about our lack of connection and I've been swimming in it all day. I am hurting and my thoughts are all over the place. Do you want me to share more?"

Now, I have cracked open my chest and you get to decide what you're going to do. If you decide to meet me halfway and we exchange more truth, that's awesome. But even if you don't, I still control my truth. I will show you my truth and demonstrate trust regardless of your actions.

Jesus manages His trust in ways that scare the pants off of most of us. Think about this—on the night His disciples would betray and abandon Him, He brought them around the Last Supper table and said, "Let's make a covenant." What kind of person says, "Hey you betrayers, come get closer, let me deepen my covenant with you right before you break yours with Me"? Someone who really knows how to manage His trust—that's who!

The Pillar of Faith

Many addiction recovery programs teach people that they need to pursue a connection with God if they want to break out of bondage from a substance or activity. This aspect of recovery acknowledges that the other side of our human instinct to avoid pain is our instinct to grab hold of things that calm our anxiety and make us feel better—things that bring us comfort, safety, and pleasure.

We have a deep, God-created need for intimacy, love, and comfort. But if we look to things that were not designed to meet these needs and elevate them above everything else—making them idols—then the result is always bondage and destruction. It's only when we place God at the center that we can access the comfort, peace, safety, joy, and pleasure that truly meets our deepest needs. Only faith in the One who made us can make us truly free.

When you put a person in the position of God, you set him or her up for failure. Think of a man who makes his wife his god. He makes her responsible for his joy, identity, and comfort—all things that only God should satisfy. Inevitably, his anxiety goes through the roof whenever he can't control her. He has put her in charge of such deep needs in his life that he becomes scared of her. She is his addiction. And when he can't get his fix, he ends up in a mess. His only hope is to turn to God. God must satisfy his needs. No one else can do that "God job" like God can.

Mysterious as it is, making ourselves accountable to God and putting ourselves under His authority is the only way we can become powerful and learn to govern ourselves. The founding fathers of the United States understood this very well. They taught that a free society is only free because individuals submit themselves by faith to divine authority and a code of virtue. The moment you remove faith from a society, you remove the possibility of self-government. When people refuse to be accountable to God, the only answer is to control them externally through systems of punishment that take away their freedom.

The pillar of faith is built in a relationship as two people commit to keep God as their ultimate source, ultimate comforter, and ultimate authority. The result of this commitment is that both people are able to govern themselves and access a boundless well of spiritual resources (wisdom, strength, love, hope, etc.) to sustain them in moving toward their relational goals. When two people are consistently pursuing a connection with the Perfect One, that connection will set the pace for their connection with each other. They will be learning to love from Love Himself, which can only bring the best into their relationship.

The pain and the fear that comes from being disconnected in a relationship usually leaves you feeling powerless to do anything about it.

Unless Sheri and I turn our attention to God after an argument, we feel controlled or despondent in our distance. Over and over again after we disconnect, we turn our attention to God until we are able to connect. Our anxiety lessens, the goal of love is reestablished, and we gain a supernatural energy to reconnect.

The Pillar of Vision

One of my favorite movies is *The Legend of Bagger Vance*. The main character, Rannulph Junuh, is a promising young golfer who takes the golf circuit by storm in the early 1900s. When World War I breaks out, he is swept away from the life, woman, and game he loves to serve his country. After the war, he returns to Savannah, Georgia as a shell of the man he once was. Completely derailed, Junuh avoids everything he used to love, surviving from one day to the next.

Then, after a series of events during the Great Depression, Junuh ends up back in the game of golf, representing Savannah in an exhibition game against the two top golfers of his day, Bobby Jones and Walter Hagen. Into this opportunity for redemption walks Bagger Vance, a Holy-Spirit-type figure who appears out of nowhere one night before the exhibition as Junuh is taking practice shots. Vance starts setting up the balls for Junuh. After a series of bad shots, Vance looks up at Junuh and says, "You loss yo swang. We's got ta help ya's fine yo swang again, Mr. Junuh." [3] With Vance's coaching, Junuh indeed finds his swing and makes a brilliant showing at the exhibition.

Junuh's "swing" is a metaphor for your identity and calling—what you were created to be and to do. As Bagger Vance did for Junuh, the Holy Spirit is committed to helping you find your "swing." But at the end of the day, *you are the one holding the club.* No one else can fulfill your potential. You have to embark on your own quest to discover why you are on this planet, what makes you get out of bed in the morning, and what you uniquely contribute to the world.

Along with a personal vision, a couple needs a shared vision if they are going to have a healthy relationship. Some couples have the vision to create the ideal "Christian marriage." Other couples want to create a 100-million-dollar business together. Others want to serve in Sudan. Whatever the goal, a shared vision is necessary in order to move together in managing your priorities and preserving unity. You do not want to be on a plane to China, meet someone during your layover in New York who is headed to Australia, fall in love, marry that person, change your flight to Australia, and decide five years later that you were supposed to be in China. Instead, just find somebody on the plane to China.

Some people never gain a vision for their identity and calling and stumble blindly and aimlessly through life, existing at the level of survival. Others do get a vision, but lose sight of it through traumatic events, as Junuh did, or through their own neglect. Proverbs 29:18 says, "Where there is no vision, the people perish." [4] One of the reasons people perish without a vision is that they cannot endure the pain and cost required to achieve any worthwhile purpose. *Only vision can give a purpose to your pain, which enables you to endure it and reach your goal.* Christ demonstrated this incredible power of vision to help us endure: "...for the joy set before Him, [He] endured the cross." [5]

One of the marks of powerful people is that they proactively establish practices and build relationships that help to renew their vision and remind them of who they are. When two people establish the pillar of vision in their relationship, they share the knowledge of one another's identity and calling, as well as their joint vision, and remind one another of these things on a regular basis. When seasons of difficulty, pain, or loss come up, the pillar of vision strengthens a relational connection and protects it from being thrown into survival mode.

Creating an Environment for Shalom

When you and another person lay a firm foundation of unconditional love and acceptance and actively build the pillars of love, honor, self-control, responsibility, truth, faith, and vision in your connection, you raise a structure that can protect and cultivate an environment of *shalom*.

Shalom is a powerful Hebrew word that encompasses the flourishing of divine order, divine health, and divine prosperity in your life. It means that every part of your life—body, soul, spirit, relationships, dreams, and work—is being nourished and is growing and thriving. Shalom is literally the reality of God's kingdom of righteousness, peace, and joy being expressed in your life.

Do you want the highest level of quality in your connections with other people? Do you want relationships that invite shalom? Then I encourage you to go after each of the architectural elements we've explored in this chapter. Examine your current thinking and behavior in each of these areas. Ask yourself, "Can my spouse or friends truly be themselves around me? Am I moving toward the people I love no matter what? Am I showing them the truth of my heart? Am I able to respond well in any situation, or do I react and blame my choices on external forces?"

Remember, nobody can manage your love but you. Nobody can manage your honor but you. Nobody can manage your truth but you. Nobody can manage your self-control or responsibility but you. And nobody can manage your vision and your faith but you.

The quality of what you are building is ultimately up to you.

Section Two

COMMUNICATION

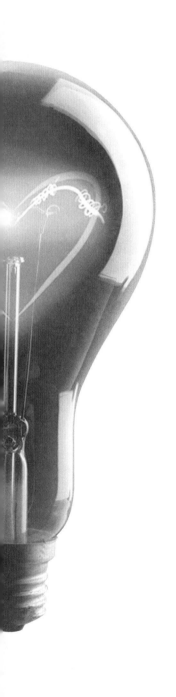

Chapter Five

COMMUNICATION: EXCHANGING THE TRUTH INSIDE

Communication exposes what is going on inside the human heart. Jesus said, "For out of the abundance of the heart the mouth speaks." [1] If your heart, your internal reality, is governed by fear, then you are going to telegraph that through your body language, facial expressions, words, and tone. Conversely, if your heart is governed by faith, hope, and love, you will release this reality through what you say and how you say it.

If your heart is governed by fear, then much of what you communicate is actually designed to hide what is *really* going on inside. You hold back, pretend something doesn't hurt, or act happy when your heart is breaking in an attempt to avoid the pain that being "real" can inflict.

It's also possible that you (like many) were never taught how to interpret and translate the language of your thoughts, emotions, and desires into words, let alone communicate them to others. As a result, your internal reality has never been validated. Now ashamed and fearful—the results of not knowing how to communicate your feelings—you hide behind an acceptable social mask.

Fear of truth is the great hijacker of communication. When you don't have either the courage or the ability to face the truth of what you feel, think, and need, you end up communicating confusing and inaccurate information—sometimes even downright falsehoods.

Ask yourself these two questions.

1   If you never really learn to value and understand what's going on inside you, how can you value and understand what is going on with another person?

2   If you don't know yourself, how can you get to know another person—someone with a completely different experience and perspective—and value the truth of who they are?

> *Fear of truth is the great hijacker of communication.*

The answer to both questions is simple. You can't.

Only those who value and understand themselves can value and understand others. Only those who can communicate honestly with themselves can communicate honestly with others.

These are both the traits of a powerful person. Unless you become a powerful person who values what is going on in your heart, your experience with communication is guaranteed to be an endless sequence of misunderstandings and being misunderstood.

Powerless people communicate out of the fear of truth, and they primarily do it in one of three styles—*passive communication, aggressive communication, or passive-aggressive communication.* As you'll see, each of these styles traces back to false core beliefs about the value of what is inside a person. Worse, they cultivate fear and destroy connection because they provide a way for people not to tell the truth.

Passive Communication

Passive communicators attempt to convince the world that everyone else is more important than they are. Their core belief is, "You matter and I don't." When faced with a joint decision in a relationship, the passive person insists that the other person's thoughts, feelings, and needs matter more. If they believe that their feelings, thoughts, and needs are being disrespected, they will simply try to absorb it and move on. Passive communicators say things like, "Oh whatever you want. No, that's okay. No, that didn't hurt. No, I'm fine. No, I know you were just upset. No, I don't need to talk about this anymore. I'm good. No, I don't care where we go—wherever you want! I'm fine. No, I'm great."

Passive people justify devaluing themselves by painting themselves as longsuffering, patient servants who keep the peace and don't ever make problems. They think it's right to have no needs or requirements.

In reality, they are lying cowards.

If I am a passive communicator, then I will lie because I am afraid of what you will do if you find out that I have needs. I'm afraid of being punished for telling the truth. I'm afraid of communicating what's going on with me, because I'm afraid you'll think I'm a bad person, or that I'm selfish. Somehow, I actually believe that it is noble to hide myself from the relationship. But I am only feeding my own anxiety by ensuring that you will never know the truth inside me. You will never be dealing with the real me. You will always be dealing with the façade.

And of course, the passive approach, being a lie, is impossible to maintain in the long term. The bitterness that grows by absorbing other people's selfishness will ultimately make passive people more miserable than scared, and so they will take action. They will stop being passive and will probably end the relationship so that their needs will finally be met.

The problem is that the passive people have been just as selfish as the ones toward whom they're bitter. They devalued their own needs, not out of a desire to benefit the other person, but out of self-protection.

I know two sisters. One lent the other a moderate sum of money. Days turned into weeks, weeks turned into months, months turned into years, and still the one sister did not pay back the sum of money. The sister who loaned the money—the ultimate passive communicator— was inwardly seething, but she never confronted her sister about it. She wanted to maintain peace. She abhorred confrontation, and since she didn't "need" the money, she did not feel that her need to be repaid was valuable enough to be addressed. Nevertheless, by year seven, she couldn't take it anymore and decided that she would just sue her sister. There is little peace in the family now. Hurt has skyrocketed on both sides, and connection might be irreparably damaged. This is not healthy communication.

Aggressive Communication

The aggressive communicator is like a T-Rex. His or her core belief is, "I matter. You don't!" Aggressive communicators know how to get what they want. They are large and in charge because they are the biggest, loudest, scariest one in the room.

If we were to line up a communication food chain, the aggressive communicator would be the T-rex at the top, and the passive communicator would be a goat cowering at the bottom. The craziest thing happens, though—the T-Rex and the goat end up in a relationship together! How in the world does this happen?

Simple. They both agree on something: the T-Rex matters and the goat doesn't. *What a pair!*

This communication dynamic sends anxiety through the roof, because the unequal value and power balance entirely eliminates intimacy. It can only be a relationship of survival. The T-Rex will get what he needs by taking it and the goat will get what she needs by giving away body parts to the T-Rex. In the end, the goat will no longer exist, and the T-Rex will still be hungry.

Both are motivated by fear and selfishness, and both are powerless.

Passive-Aggressive Communication

The passive-aggressive communication style is the most sophisticated, and therefore the most devious of the fear-based communication styles. It is the worst of being passive and the worst of being aggressive.

The passive-aggressive communicator's core belief is: "You matter… No, not really!" They manipulate and control others through active deceit and subtle-but-deadly forms of punishment. To your face they say, "Oh, whatever you need, absolutely." Then, after your little disagreement, they head outside and key your car. The passive-aggressive communicator is famous for sarcastic innuendos, veiled threats, the manipulative use of Scriptures, judgments that come in the form of counsel, and withholding love.

Because passive-aggressive communicators maintain a veneer of civility, it is often hard for people on the outside to understand why someone has such a difficult time being in relationship with them. Someone who is trying to gain counsel about dealing with a passive-aggressive person looks crazy, because he or she is the only one who perceives all the person's hostility and manipulation. To everyone else, the passive-aggressive person is kind and bubbly and smiling all the time. They don't know that the second they get behind closed doors, he or she is insinuating, criticizing, accusing, stonewalling, and sending mixed messages that would drive anyone insane.

I describe a passive-aggressive communicator as a "chocolate-covered dragon." Sometimes women are attracted to men who appear charming and romantic, flatter them incessantly, and who are just plain too good to be true. It's not until women get into deeper relationships with these passive-aggressive men that they learn that they are actually chocolate-covered dragons. Once the "nice" façade is gone, they become vicious manipulators who discount these women's thoughts and feelings. They are often jealous of anything the women do that doesn't revolve around them.

I once knew a chocolate-covered dragon who happened to be a pastor. He had an argument with a member of the congregation who was also a friend of his wife. In the midst of their argument, this friend mentioned that she wanted to help the pastor's wife work through an issue. The pastor responded, "If my wife wanted help with this problem she would go talk to somebody she trusts and respects." He was not saying what his wife felt about this woman. He was saying how *he* felt about her in a devious way. Both his dislike and his insinuations inflicted pain. That is passive aggression, and it can be devastating.

Assertive Communication

> *The core belief of assertive communicators is, "You matter and so do I."*

So if these are the communication styles that grow out of being powerless and afraid of the truth, what communication style grows out of being powerful and loving the truth? The answer is ***assertive communication.***

The core belief of assertive communicators is, "You matter and so do I. My thoughts, feelings, and needs matter, and so do yours." Assertive communicators refuse to have relationships or conversations where both people do not have a high, equal value. They are not afraid to show the other person what is happening inside them. Because they value what is inside them, they take the time and effort to understand their thoughts, feelings, and needs, and to find words to express them clearly and honestly. This process enhances their ability to value and understand what another person communicates to them about his or her own heart. This is the core value of honor and mutual respect. This is the value assertive communicators protect as they interact.

Assertive communicators are unafraid of being powerful *and* letting other people be powerful within a relationship or a conversation. In fact, they insist on having two powerful people in every conversation. They refuse to give in to the temptation to turn into a T-Rex, a chocolate-covered dragon, or a goat, and they confront other people if they see them slipping into those roles.

A powerful assertive communicator responds to a passive person with, "What are you going to do about it?"

They respond to an aggressive person with, "I can only talk with you when you decide to be respectful."

And they respond to a passive-aggressive person with, "We can talk later when you choose to be responsible and tell me what is really going on."

In other words, they are able to set consistent boundaries around a conversation so that it stays respectful, and they require both participants to equally participate in pursuing the goal of the conversation.

The First Goal of Conversation: Understanding, not Agreement

Some people think that talking is communicating. But talking is not communicating unless it has a goal, a purpose. Most often in communication, the goal is agreement. But if our goal is agreement, then what happens when we disagree? I must persuade you to agree with me, or vice versa. But unfortunately, persuasion has a way of slipping into pressure, manipulation, and control. The priority of agreement demands that there really can't be two different people in the conversation— there can only be one. The longer you refuse to respond to my efforts to convince you to agree with me, the more anxiety grows in the conversation. Before long, the battle lines are drawn and we are allowing our need to be right to overtake our need to protect our connection. The conversation becomes a fight over which one of us has the *right* perception, the *right* answer, or the *right* decision.

If we are not careful, it will be only a matter of time before one of us introduces some kind of "relationship killer" to the conversation. A relationship killer is a message that invalidates or disqualifies one person's thoughts, feelings, or needs in some way. It most often happens when someone mentions his or her feelings and the other person responds:

"Well, that's not logical. You can't be right because you just have a feeling. We can't measure your feelings. We have to present things logically. Your 'feeling' doesn't even make sense. My perspective, on the other hand, has all the qualifiers to be valuable." The underlying message, although unintended, is, "I am valuable and you are not." When people start devaluing one another's thoughts, feelings, or needs in some way, they are attacking their connection like a pack of wolves.

If connection is the priority, then the goal of communication cannot be agreement, because then one person has to disappear when there is disagreement. And guess what? People do not always agree. If we want to keep two powerful people involved and connected in a conversation, the first goal in the conversation must be to *understand*. The person whose goal is to understand says, "I want to understand your unique perspective and experience. I want to understand the truth of what is happening inside you. And I want you to understand the same things about me. If I understand your heart, then I can move toward you in ways that build our connection. I can respond to your thoughts, respect your feelings, and help to meet your needs."

> *If we want to keep two powerful people involved and connected in a conversation, the first goal must be to understand.*

The results of this conversation are going to be radically different from the one whose goal was agreement alone. Pursuing the goal of understanding will help you progress through increasingly deeper levels of honesty in order to build true intimacy and trust in a relationship.

Moving From Facts and Clichés to Feelings and Needs

When we are first getting to know someone, our conversations are usually centered on the world around us. We exchange facts and clichés, such as the following:

"How are you?"

"Fine. How are you?"

"Great. What's new?"

"Not much. Beautiful day."

"Sure is."

"Supposed to be 80 degrees today. It says so right here in the paper."

"Oh, look at that."

This conversation requires a very minimal level of connection or vulnerability—you could probably have it with an absolute stranger. Sadly, there are many people who camp out at the level of facts and clichés in their relationships. It's comfortable and safe. They usually choose to do this because when they tried to graduate to the next level of intimacy in communication in the past, they got scared and hurt. They ended up in those big, long, disrespectful, "relationship killer" conversations and got so burned that they decided it was safer to retreat to communication that required no vulnerability or risk whatsoever. They use communication to pursue the goal of distance and disconnection rather than connection.

The only way you can build a heart-to-heart connection with someone is to communicate on a heart level about your feelings and needs. This is the level where we express vulnerability and build trust. This is the level where we get in touch with the truth about who we are and how we affect people around us.

Perhaps you have heard the joke about the man who goes to the doctor and complains about suffering from terrible constant gas. "But it's the weirdest thing, doctor," he says. "I don't make a sound and it doesn't smell."

The doctor looks at him and says bluntly, "Okay. Well, the first thing we are going to do is get you hearing aids. And then we are going to figure out what's wrong with your nose."

This is what many of us experience every day when we try to communicate. There is a lot going on around us that we don't always pick up. Sometimes we are completely unaware of how other people are "experiencing" us.

I love to tell people about how my wife experiences the way I drive up Buckhorn Mountain on my way to Weaverville, CA. This stretch of road features superb twists and turns that are perfect for weaving in and out of traffic. The risk of plummeting hundreds of feet to your death lies only a few feet away. When I'm driving, I fly around those corners, passing every car I can overtake. It is marvelous!

My wife always has a completely different experience on these drives than I do—an experience I don't understand. I am a good driver, as evidenced by the fact that I have never been in an accident. Personally, I think I should have been a NASCAR driver or at least signed up for a car rally.

When she lets me know that she feels scared as I am driving, I always think, *Why are you scared? You have absolutely no evidence that I am a bad driver. You should just calm down and be like me.*

But as mystifying as it is, I know my wife is not like me, and I cannot make her be like me. I can't force her to feel what I feel and know what I know. I trust her to believe the best about me, so I know that when she tells me she is scared, she is not insinuating that I am trying to scare her. She is simply telling me what she feels.

If I were to argue with Sheri's feelings, I would devalue her. "You shouldn't feel that way. There's no valid reason for you to feel like that. I don't feel like that. Change and be like me." This thought process is as ridiculous as someone saying, "I'm hungry," and responding, "No you're not! I'm not hungry so you can't be hungry." How silly is that? But that is exactly what we do when we respond to others without taking the time to understand, appreciate, and validate their feelings.

When I value your feelings, I will not only make it safe for you to communicate them to me, but I will also listen and respond. I will invite you to go deeper and show me what it is you need, so we can move from understanding to decision-making and action.

Understanding one another's needs is the Holy Grail of communication. If I can find out what you need in a conversation and find out how to satisfy that need, then it changes everything!

A drastic turning point in my marriage with Sheri came when she discovered (through inner healing) that she had a deep need to feel protected by me, a need she had never previously identified. Unsurprisingly, it was a need that had never been met in our relationship. It had never occurred to me that she had this need because she had been working to meet that need herself—usually by protecting herself from me.

When Sheri told me what she had discovered, I was offended. I had always felt like I was the victim and she the aggressive offender in our relationship. I blamed her for the fact that I was not courageous. In fifteen years of marriage, I had never—not once—thought it was my job to protect Sheri. She had always appeared so self-sufficient. But the Lord confronted me and told me she was right. She needed me to protect her. I listened to God and permanently changed the way I responded to her. At first, she didn't trust me, but after a while she realized that I was going to stick it out. This took us to totally new places of vulnerability and radically changed our relationship. Her former levels of anxiety dropped dramatically and our connection strengthened exponentially—all because I can now meet this need in her.

The faster you can get to the question, "What do you need?" the faster you can start doing something about it. Unfortunately, because many people are not used to being listened to, they don't know what they need, or how to communicate it. They think they to have to present a solid case for someone to help them, agree with them, or change for them.

For many years, Sheri was a pastor at the Bethel School of Supernatural Ministry and frequently had students come into her office to deal with some issue, their emotions flying everywhere. Quietly, she would ask them, "Hey, what do you need?"

This question always shocked them. "What?" they'd reply.

"What is it that you need?" Sheri repeated.

Then it would dawn on them. "I don't even know what I need. Oh my gosh!"

I have also found that people are usually thrown off guard when I simply show up with the question, "What do you need? Tell me so I can help you with that." It has never crossed their mind that I would help simply because they need something. As soon as they experience it, they immediately recognize it as a practice of intimacy. They feel cared for and loved, which casts out anxiety and helps the search for the truth of what their heart needs.

You can start practicing the skills of assertive communication by paying attention to your thoughts, feelings, and needs and respecting their value. Then start doing the same for other people. Check yourself when you are tempted to invalidate someone's experience or heart. Listen to understand in a conversation—especially to understand what a person is feeling and what he or she needs. Seek healing from past experiences that have led you to fear the truth of your heart and become a passive, aggressive, or passive-aggressive communicator. Be real with yourself. If you start slipping into your old styles of communication, then do what needs to be done to make things right.

When you commit to becoming the best communicator you could possibly be, you commit to connection, and to being a truly powerful person. Not only will your relationship with your heart change for the better, but your relationships with others will be transformed.

Chapter Six

THE TRUST CYCLE

I n the book of Mathew, Jesus said that it is better for someone to tie an enormous rock around your neck, kick you into the deepest part of the ocean, and let you sink, rather than allow you to cause a child to stumble.[1] Apparently, protecting the trust of the vulnerable is a big deal to Jesus—and for good reason. When people mess with your trust at an early age, you are likely to struggle in life. Most gang members, high school dropouts, and addicts had bad childhoods. Most abusers were abused. Most divorcées had divorced parents. Affairs, selfishness, self-inflicted pain, and walls of protection all stem from broken trust during childhood.

We were designed to live out of trust. In fact, psychologists argue that trust is the first developmental task every person must achieve in infancy in order to develop a healthy sense of personhood and to develop healthy relationships.[2] When babies come out of the womb, the first question their little hearts and minds asks is, "Can I trust the world?" The answer to this question comes as the primary caregiver meets—or fails to meet—their physical and emotional needs.

Babies, like anyone else, have needs. In fact, needs are about all a baby has. And the only thing babies can do to let the world know what they need is to cry. They cry when they are hungry or tired, when they need a diaper changed, when they need to burp, and when they need to be held. When they cry and a need is met, a trust cycle is completed. They learn that they can trust themselves—the signals they are sending are understood—and they learn to trust the person meeting their needs.

This trust cycle can *only* be completed through a relational connection, because only a relationship can meet the full range of a baby's needs. If babies are fed, clothed, and washed, but never experience prolonged human touch, cuddling, and face-to-face contact with their primary caregiver, their brains, personalities, and capacity for bonding will remain underdeveloped—and in some cases permanently stunted.

From the moment we enter the world, our deepest need is to love and be loved by other human beings and to engage in lasting relational bonds. Our ability to meet this need develops as we consistently complete trust cycles in our interactions with other people. A trust cycle is completed when you:

1   Have a need

2   The need is expressed

3   There is a response to the need

4   The need is satisfied

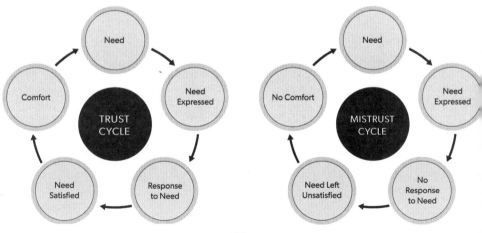

Here is the problem—this trust cycle can break down at any point. Trust is damaged if people fail to identify and express their needs, if the other person does not respond to the need or responds in a negative way, or if the need is not ultimately met.

Of course, we all experience broken trust in life. Most of us experience it in childhood, simply because all parents, even the best of them, are human beings who make mistakes and bring their own areas of brokenness into parenting. And if these wounds are not healed and truth and trust restored, they will fester, damaging our ability to create intimacy in relationships.

Painful experiences give way to wounds that fester when we agree with lies like:

God doesn't love me.

No one loves me.

There's something wrong with me, and that's why I'm unworthy of love.

That person would never love me if they really knew me.

I don't deserve to have my needs met.

Sound familiar?

Agreement with these lies creates an *expectation* for unmet needs. That expectation leads us into more painful, disappointing experiences, and prevents the wound from ever healing.

If you have gone through counseling or inner healing, you know how just one bad experience or one empowered lie can bring significant pain and relational handicaps into your life. For people who grew up in environments where they consistently experienced neglect or punishment in response to their needs, the damage is significant. The cycle of mistrust creates an alienating, painful reality where people feel hopeless about ever having their needs met because they are unable to trust others and form strong relational connections. These people, cut off from love, become survivors.

Survivors learn to manipulate their environment and other people in order to get *some* of their needs met. They don't expect to be loved, because after years of abandonment, neglect, and abuse, they believe they are unworthy of love. They don't expect relationships to last—why should they? They are not anyone's beloved. It's never been safe for them to trust or be vulnerable. And they certainly don't have the emotional resources to try to meet anyone else's needs. So they will take what they can get.

And what do you know? Survivors end up creating a reality where they are not loved, relationships don't last, and the pain of unmet needs continues to destroy their lives.

This is hallmark of the orphan spirit—the very spirit from which God sent His Son to deliver us.

Jesus' comment about how serious it is to cause a child to stumble reveals the jealous, protective love of the Father for His lost, orphaned children—which includes all of us. Jesus went to the Cross to avenge the stolen innocence and broken trust we all inherited after the Fall. When He declared that we all had to be "born again," He was saying, "We're going to start this trust thing over again. I'm placing you in the Father's arms, where you are going to experience unconditional love, acceptance, and care. He is going to meet your needs when you cry out to Him— especially your need to be loved. You're going to learn how to trust again. And you're going to be able to build relationships with Me and one another, relationships where your heart will be satisfied."

There is no one too broken or too far gone with an orphan spirit that he or she cannot come home to the Father's house to live and love as God designed.

That is the heart of the Gospel—and that is truly good news.

Expressing Our Needs

Expressing our needs and building relational connections are closely intertwined—in fact; they are completely dependent on one another.

As I explained in the last chapter, the level of communication we need to reach in order to build a strong relational connection is the level where we express our needs to one another. It's no mistake that this is exactly where the trust cycle begins. You simply can't build a strong bond of trust without being able to communicate and meet one another's needs.

If you cannot communicate your needs to another person clearly, it is obviously going to be very difficult for that person to meet them. That's why one of the primary tasks of reaching maturity is learning how to express thoughts, feelings, and needs. Those who never learn this skill, however, expect relationships to function without it. They say things like, "Well, if you love me, then you will just *know* what I need. Didn't you notice that that bothered me? Haven't you been paying attention? I can't believe you don't know that about me."

Where does this desire or expectation that loved ones have a telepathic ability to know our feelings and needs come from? It comes from powerlessness and fear. It comes from dreaming that everything will turn out magically without actually having to *communicate*. Powerless people want to win the lottery, get their dream girl/guy with minimal effort, lose weight without exercise, and get their needs met without ever having to say a word.

Yeah, well…powerless people, prepare yourselves for what I'm about to tell you:

It just doesn't work that way.

The reason we can't get our needs met without expressing them is that we were designed to have our needs met through a relational exchange. God made us this way. This is how He meets our needs. Think about it. God, the one Person in the universe who knows all things, and knows us incomparably better than we know ourselves, never says, "Well, obviously I know your needs, so you don't need to tell me about them." Instead, He repeatedly tells us to ask Him for what we need, and gives us some of the most profound, beautiful, and honest language for doing so—like the Lord's Prayer, and most of the Psalms. He won't meet our needs outside of a connection where we have to show up and crack our hearts open to Him, because that very connection is what we need to have our needs met in the first place.

If God Himself respects our prerogative as individuals to make our feelings, needs, and desires known to Him in a relationship, then we may take it that this is how He designed us to relate with one another. In a respectful relationship, each person understands, "I am responsible to know what is going on inside me and communicate it to you. I do not expect you to know it, nor will I allow you to assume that you know it. And I will not make assumptions about what is going on inside you."

Conversely, the belief that other people can know you, or that you can know others, without needing to willingly disclose your hearts to one another is inherently disrespectful, and will lead you to act in ways that damage trust. As long as you believe this, the line of demarcation between your life and another person's life will remain fuzzy, leading you to avoid taking responsibility for communicating what is going on inside you, and to wrongly take responsibility for telling other people what is going on inside them.

Unfortunately, this wrong belief infects most relational communication. So many people think, "If I'm in a relationship with you, then I get to tell you about you." Yet what inevitably happens when they act on this?

"Here, let me tell you about you. This is what you are thinking and feeling. This is what you need. These are your motives."

Comments like this are inherently judgmental, presumptuous, and disrespectful—even if offered in a kind tone and with the best of intentions. And unless the person on the receiving end of such comments knows how to set a boundary with disrespect, he or she will usually go into self-protective mode and either shut down or begin retaliating in kind—"So you're going to tell me about me, huh? Okay, then I get to tell you about you." The ensuing duel of judgments is sure to damage any relational connection. If you want to protect your connection and build trust by always communicating respectfully, then your guiding rule must be, "It's my job to tell you about me, and your job to tell me about you."

"I" Messages

The best tool for telling another person about you is an "I message." The basic structure of the "I message" is: "I feel [emotion] when [describe experience] and I need to feel [emotion]."

Notice that the "I message" begins with "*I feel*," not "*I think*." The "I message" is designed to let other people know what is happening inside you, not for you to let them know what you think about them or what you think they need to do. As you construct an "I message," make sure that you are really expressing a feeling, not an opinion.

"I feel like you are a jerk," is not a feeling. It is an opinion—because you could replace "feel like" with "think."

If you start to say, "I feel *like*..." you should stop and check yourself—because what is most likely going to follow is not a feeling, but a judgment. And a judgment statement is actually an expression of mistrust, not trust. A judgment statement says, "I'm too scared to show you what is really going on inside me. I'll only feel safe to show you what I'm feeling if you first agree with my assessment of what's wrong with you and then promise never to be like that again."

> An "I message" is: "I feel [emotion] when [describe experience] and I need to feel [emotion]."

Nothing guarantees raising another person's defenses and hijacking a conversation more than a judgment statement. In their fear, people convince themselves that they can make people change without needing to be vulnerable, rather than trusting people to change by offering vulnerability. These conversations sound something like, "Honey can I talk to you? Can we share our hearts? Can we just...have a conversation?

Please, please don't get defensive, but I need to share my heart with you. Will you hear it with love? 'Cause this is the truth with love, right here. Here it comes. Ready? Honey, now listen, listen, please listen. Hear my heart. Well, I feel like you *are selfish and evil.*"

And for some weird reason, they expect the other person to go, "Thank you! I was wondering what was wrong with me!"

Yeah. That never happens.

Instead, we need to take the approach that says, "I feel a feeling and it's connected to an event. When this happened, this is the feeling that I had. And I need to feel something different than what is happening."

For example:

"I feel scared when you drive this fast. I need to feel safe and protected when I am in the car with you."

"I need to hear about you and feel valued when we talk."

"I feel hurt when you talk to me like that."

"I feel hurt and judged when you frame it like this."

"When you hit the wall in anger, I feel scared."

"I feel rejected when you react to my efforts to help you like that."

When you send "I messages" like these, you let the other person see your true emotions. Then he or she can decide how to respond. You become vulnerable and powerful, because you protect the other person's choice to move toward you and meet your needs on their own terms.

If you're on the receiving end of the "I message," you have some decisions to make:

1   Are you going to honor the vulnerability offered, value the person's need, and figure out how you can meet it?

2   Are you going to be powerful enough to adjust yourself in order to move toward the person and protect your connection and trust?

Both of these choices often require at least as much vulnerability as it took for the other person to show you his or her need. It is vulnerable (scary and humbling) to allow someone's needs to influence your heart and your actions. But know this—doing your part to complete the trust cycle is just as important for you as for the other person. *One of your needs in a relationship is to be able to meet the other person's needs!* You need them to receive your love. And you need to know that you are a powerful, trustworthy person who can choose to grow, change, adjust, and do what you need to do to love people in ways they can receive. It will do wonders for your self-respect.

Made For Intimacy and Freedom

A safe place for intimacy is created when two people can express their needs and consistently complete the trust cycle for one another in a relationship. Intimacy—"into-me-see"—is created between two people who can say, "We can be ourselves together because you can see into me and I can see into you." The experience of intimacy—of being completely known and accepted, and completely knowing and accepting in return—is the most satisfying experience we can have as humans. Intimacy in a safe place brings *euphoria*. Remember the Garden of Eden? Paradise was the place where a man and a woman were free to be vulnerable and intimate with one another in every way.

The problem is that most of us are scared to death to be vulnerable in relationships. The reason is simple: In being vulnerable, we reach for our greatest need while risking our greatest pain. If acceptance brings euphoria, then rejection brings shame and heartbreak. And by the time most of us reach adulthood, we have had enough painful experiences with rejection that risking our hearts is a serious struggle and one most of us avoid at all costs. The lie that we are inherently unworthy to be loved convinces many of us that hiding is our only option. And because we're hiding, we want everyone else to hide too. We can't handle the truth

> *Intimacy—
> "into-me-see"*

of who they are any more than we can handle the truth of who we are. If most of us were dropped into the Garden of Eden naked and saw other people running around naked, it wouldn't feel like paradise to us at all. We would freak out and want everyone to cover up as quickly as possible. We just cannot handle the idea of being exposed.

Unfortunately, fear of rejection and shame sets us up to fall for the enemy's counterfeits. Ever since sin entered the world and humanity became disconnected from God, we have been looking for ways to get our needs met outside of relationship or any scenario where we are required to be vulnerable and risk our hearts. We have always desperately sought the benefits of intimacy without wanting to pay the price. And the enemy continues to offer us the euphoric experiences we think we can control—things like alcohol, drugs, sex, Internet pornography, shopping, carbohydrates, adrenaline, or cash. You use these things to give yourself a euphoric release and take care of your needs.

But the counterfeits always have ugly repercussions, like drunk drivers killing innocent people, young kids destroying their brains, men ignoring the beautiful real women beside them in favor of images, serious debt, morbid obesity and the host of diseases that accompany it, thrill seekers slowly becoming numb to reality, and selfish jerks not caring who they step on to get what they want. Counterfeits never come through. They are the perpetual carrot in front of the horse's nose, promising love, but always out of reach.

Whenever you try to get your needs met through control, you end up being controlled and addicted. You lose your freedom. You enter into bondage that prevents the pain you are trying to self-medicate from ever being healed.

We were made to have our needs met through relationships with people we don't control. Love—a free choice—is the only thing that will satisfy our hearts. This is why the counterfeits never live up to their promises. This is why all of us must face our fear of rejection, be healed of shame, and risk our hearts in relationships. We must be willing to offer the truth of who we are to those we love, and receive the truth of who they are. Only the truth can make us free.

Chapter Seven

COMMUNICATING IN CONFLICT

W hen two people choose to walk together in relationship, there is never a question of whether or not they will experience conflict. Believe me, they will. The question is whether they will know what is at stake when conflict happens. The "thing" at stake, if you are curious, is the health of the relational connection.

Conflict is to a relationship what disease or injury is to a body. As with physical health, the goal in a relationship should be to prevent as much conflict as possible. However, in the same way that fighting off a disease or doing therapy after an injury can strengthen your body, passing through the flames of conflict in a healthy, productive way can strengthen a relational connection. It is possible to end up on the other side of conflict as more powerful individuals, freer to be yourselves, more confident in your love for each other, and more hopeful about your ability to meet each other's needs. This positive outcome is dependent, however, on what you choose to do. Will you allow conflict to tear your connection apart? Or will you fight for your connection in the midst of conflict?

Building A Conflict-Resistant Connection

To recap, here are the core values and guidelines of healthy communication:

❖ Our first goal in a conversation is to understand one another.

❖ My thoughts, feelings, and needs are valuable and important, and so are yours.

❖ I do not participate in disrespectful conversations. When my thoughts, feelings, and needs are devalued in a conversation, I will stop the conversation and set a clear boundary. Until respect is restored, I will not participate.

❖ We need to communicate our true feelings and needs to establish trust and intimacy.

❖ It's my job to tell you what is going on inside me, and your job to tell me what's going on inside you. We do not have powers of telepathy or the right to assume we know one another's motives, thoughts, feelings, or needs.

> *Our first goal in a conversation is to understand one another.*

❖ The best way to communicate my feelings and needs to you is to use "I messages" and clear, specific statements that show what I am feeling and experiencing.

❖ I will not expect you to know my feelings and needs unless I have communicated them to you.

❖ I will not make judgment statements or tell you how you must change in order to meet my needs.

❖ When you communicate your needs to me, it is my job to listen well so I can understand what you need, how my life is affecting you, and what I can do to meet your needs.

❖ I am committed to protecting and nurturing our connection. I will do what I need to do in order to keep moving toward you—no matter what.

❖ It's my job to manage my heart so that I can respond to you in love and cast out fear in our relationship.

These core values and tools of communication will prevent most conflict in relationships. Every time you express your needs, set a boundary, listen, meet a need, or speak in one another's love languages, you are nourishing and exercising your connection, keeping it healthy and resistant to harm. Yes, healthy communication often feels like hard work. A vulnerable, honest conversation requires as much energy from your mind and heart as a tough session at the gym. But the benefits of building a strong connection are even more rewarding than the rewards of building a strong body. This is where the promise of Scripture comes into play:

> *Two are better than one, because they have a good return for their labor: If either of them falls down, one can help the other up. But pity anyone who falls and has no one to help them up. Also, if two lie down together, they will keep warm. But how can one keep warm alone? Though one may be overpowered, two can defend themselves. A cord of three strands is not quickly broken.*[1]

So, how strong do you want your cord—your connection—to be? What level of difficulty do you want to prepare your relationship to withstand? What are some of the tests you may be required to face? Answering these questions will help you stay focused and intentional as you keep your relationship "in shape." Just like people trying to get lean and healthy, you need to have a goal, and need to regularly remind yourself of what's at stake in meeting that goal to sustain your motivation.

It's so easy, when things seem to be moving along well in a relationship, to ease off the gas and coast. "Well, I got her flowers yesterday and I told her I loved her. That should do me for about a week, right?" Too many days like this is like eating too many donuts.

One day you get up and realize, "Wow, I feel so far away from you. What happened?" You just got lazy, that's all. And though it may not hurt you today, someday soon a conflict is going to pull on that cord of connection, and you're going to want it to be strong. So don't back off from brave communication strength-training. If you can pass the test of prioritizing your connection when seas are calm, then you'll be ready to pass that test in the storm. You won't have to worry about that cord becoming so fragile that it breaks under the slightest pressure.

Jesus communicated in ways that intentionally tested His connections with people. He confronted people with truth that He knew they would probably reject. Remember when He announced, "He who eats My flesh and drinks My blood abides in Me, and I in him"? [2] That one deeply controversial statement was enough to get an entire crowd to walk away from their connection with Him. Only the twelve stuck around. Then He asked them, "How about you guys? Are you going to disconnect too?"

"Well, we can't promise that it didn't cross our minds, but where are we going to go? You have life."

The disciples held on to their connection with Jesus, even though they had as many theological and intellectual disagreements with His outrageous words as did every other Jew who heard them. They might have even struggled with the idea of eating Jesus' body and drinking His blood while they shared the Passover meal with Him in the upper room. After all, the true significance of Jesus' words was not unveiled until after His death and resurrection. Yet, despite this and many other mysteries Jesus threw at His disciples, they stayed with Him.

Jesus purposely created opportunities for His followers to prioritize their connection above offense, confusion, or disagreement. He knew they needed practice if they were going to protect their connection to the end. Connection with Him was more important than being right. He taught them how to hold on to the most powerful Person in the universe no matter what, and as a result, they turned the world upside down.

Sheri and I both affirm that learning to pass the test of connection in the midst of conflict has made us more powerful as individuals and given us a stronger connection than we could have ever imagined.

Remember that infamous compatibility test? It didn't lie. On the third day of our honeymoon, we started to realize just how different we were. Our immediate reaction was, "Oh my gosh, I can't believe you're like this. I'm not like that. I don't think like that. I would never say that. You scare me! Change and be like me." Finally, after many years of demonstrating that being afraid of one another and trying to change each other was both futile and fatal to our connection, we changed our priorities. We started to say, "Yeah, you are a completely different person than I am. But you get to be you and I get to be me in this relationship. What do you need? How can I help you with that?"

To this day, Sheri and I fall at opposite ends of the spectrum when it comes to personality and temperament. Her needs are very different than mine. Communicating and meeting our needs has required major adjustments and growth in both of us. But after years of responding to one another's needs in love rather than reacting in fear, we have built a connection that is strong enough to face any potential conflict. We went from being relational pudgy weaklings to champion body-builders. And while that took some time, I honestly cannot imagine anything that has the power to break us apart now.

When Conflict Gets Ugly

Conflict becomes dangerously ugly when we react out of fear and pain. Fear feeds conflict because it is in every way opposed to connection. When you can recognize what happens when your natural defenses are triggered by a perceived threat, you can put a plan of action in place to get fear under control and minimize the damage to your connection.

Imagine the following scenario. Out of the blue, someone you know approaches you and says, "Hey…We need to talk." Are you hit with racing thoughts and a racing heartbeat? Do you get angry? Do you stay out of sight, try to weasel your way out of the conversation, make excuses, and dance around the issue? Or do you just shut down? Again, these are all those classic fear reactions—fight, flight, or freeze. And all of them will damage your connection if you let them.

Sure, the damage is obvious when you get two fighters together and they turn a verbal spat into drag-out mortal combat. But it's just as ugly when you get two "flight" people running away from one another, telling lies, and pretending everything is all right. And then there are the "freezers" who simply refuse to engage and turn off their love. It may not look violent, but when you look at how it poisons and starves the life out of a connection, it is definitely ugly.

In the early years of our marriage, Sheri was a fighter and I was a freezer. When she was hurt or scared, Sheri went into T-Rex mode. When I saw T-Rex coming at me, I turned into a clam. Needless to say, a conversation between a T-Rex and a clam is not going to be productive. The only thing that came out of those confrontations was enough frustration and hurt to put our connection in the hospital. Resolution was categorically impossible.

If you want to avoid ugly, you must have a plan for how you are going to respond when someone pushes that giant red button on your chest and invites you into a duel. There is a real chance that the person who pushed that button is already under the influence of fear, pain, and anger, and may not be ready to manage themselves well in the conversation.

Shocking, I know.

People always ask me, "But, what if they don't play by the rules? What if they are mean?" In case you failed to notice, scared, hurting people do not play fair. It can be quite disturbing to see fear turn someone who is normally kind and calm into someone who is treacherous, spiteful, and violent. But that is what the spirit of fear does—it brings out the worst in us.

If you want to protect your connection, then you need to learn to defuse fear bombs and constantly steer would-be duels into respectful conversations. Only a respectful conversation is going to be productive in resolving a conflict. Remember, it is your responsibility to set a boundary for how many disrespectful, unproductive, or damaging exchanges you will endure. The moment you pick up the dueling sword, you are equally guilty for whatever blood is shed.

I Care About Your Needs

In order to steer a duel toward a respectful conversation, you need to know what a respectful conversation is. A respectful conversation has a goal, and it has a process for achieving that goal. If the other person refuses to agree to that goal and engage in that process, the conversation will fail in the "respectful" category.

The goal of a respectful conversation is to strengthen your relational connection by discovering what a person needs and how you can meet that need. However, getting a hurt and scared person to show you what they need can be tricky. Often, the first issue you'll need to confront is their belief that you do not care about their needs. As I mentioned before, this is the belief I first work to expose when people come to me with a problem. I simply ask, "What do you need?" If they anticipated that I would not care about their need, this catches them off guard. They planned to try to convince me to care without even telling me what is going on first. Instead of communicating a problem, they planned to communicate a solution.

It's pretty impossible to create a solution to a problem if you don't know what the problem is. And you're not going to identify the problem unless you are willing to admit what you need and trust me to care about that need when you show it to me. This is where people must confront their deepest fears of vulnerability and rejection. It's not easy, but true conflict resolution—the kind that heals and strengthens a relational connection—will not be achieved without it. Trying to convince someone to care about your needs without being vulnerable enough to communicate them is an exercise in futility, yet so many people fall into this fear-driven pattern.

See if you can relate to this situation. A wife has been stewing all day about how she feels disconnected and unloved by her husband. He walks in the door from a long day at work and sets his keys on the counter. He sees her, lying in wait like a lion about to attack its prey. A little unnerved, the husband takes a step into the trap.

"Honey, what's the matter?"

"Nothing."

"What do you mean nothing? That response makes me feel like you're angry with me."

"I'm not angry."

"Well, you seem angry. What's bugging you? Did something happen today?"

"No. I don't want to talk about it."

"Talk about what?"

"Nothing."

"Are we going to do this all night?"

"Oh, like you care. All you ever do is come home and ask me couple things about my day, but you never really listen. You have no idea what I have to deal with at home all day with the kids, cooking, and cleaning. All you ever do is go golfing with your buddies. You don't care about anybody but yourself!"

"Huh? Uh, honey, how long have you been feeling this way?"

"Yeah, like you care. When was the last time you told me that you loved me?"

"Uh…"

"Of course, you can't remember. I didn't think you could. When's the last time you got me flowers?"

"There was that one time…"

"Yeah, I didn't think so. You want to know when? Before we got married, that's when. I remember. You don't care. I don't even know why I'm talking to you."

She storms out and he is left wondering how in the world all this happened. The next day, he comes home with flowers and says, "I love you." But it doesn't fix the problem.

"The only reason you brought me these is because I told you to!"

That's a pretty nasty picture. You will never find a resolution when communication looks like this. The wife is afraid because her needs aren't getting met, and her needs aren't getting met because she is afraid to communicate them. When she gets her husband to act by coercion, it can't meet her need, because her real need can only be met by a free act of love. The only way she can show him the real problem is to overcome her fear, trust that he cares about her, and tell him what she needs.

The Blu-ray and the TV

Communicating the message, "I care about your needs," at the *beginning* of a respectful conversation is crucial. The next step is discovering what the need is through the process of sending and receiving clear messages to one another. In order for this process to be successful, you must have both a speaker and a *listener*. If either component is missing, you either have silence or a collective monologue, not a conversation.

I like to illustrate this process with a TV and a DVD player. Imagine that you have a beautiful 60-inch, flat-screen, 3-D television and a top-of-the-line Blu-ray disc player. In order for this entertainment system to work, you need all the correct cables plugged into the right spots. When you put your favorite movie in the Blu-ray player, it will read its contents and send the information through the cables to the TV. The TV will then interpret that information and turn it into images.

In a respectful conversation, one of you is the Blu-ray player and the other is the TV. It's very important that you only play one of these roles at a time, or you will end up with a processing error. If you are the Blu-ray player, your job is to read the contents of your thoughts, feelings, and needs, and send a clear message about those contents to the TV. The TV's job is to receive that message and display it back to you. Only when you both agree that the message has been successfully communicated and understood can you switch roles or begin to discuss solutions.

Of course, we're humans, not machines, so sending and receiving messages to one another is going to be a little more dynamic and take a little more time and effort. As the Blu-ray player, you might struggle to read the "disc" of what is going on inside you (especially if you are dealing with fear and don't have a lot of practice identifying your needs). You're probably going to throw out a bunch of messages to the TV that are still in some kind of jumbled code. The TV person's job is to help you decipher that code by asking questions: "Is this what you're saying? Is this the message you want me to receive? Is this what you are feeling?" None of these questions should be asked or interpreted as judgments, but as honest attempts to clarify what you, the Blu-ray player, have said. As you hear the TV feeding back your message to you, you'll be able to identify discrepancies and make corrections: "No, that's not what I was trying to say at all. Let me try this again. I actually feel…"

In a respectful conversation, one of you is the Blu-ray player and the other is the TV.

As the Blu-ray player, it's your responsibility to stick to reading your "disc" and not offer your opinions and judgments of the TV. The minute you start to say, "You this, you that," the connection cables are in danger of shorting out.

If you're the TV on the receiving end of a "you" attack, you might try to give the Blu-ray player a pass and see if they are willing to reframe their "you" message as an 'I message.'

"All right, so you sound scared and hurt when this happens. Is that what you are saying?"

"No I'm not scared! I'm mad!"

"All right, but you are probably mad because you don't have control over this. Is that what you're saying?"

"Yes, I don't have any control!"

"Okay, well, what are you going to do about that? How can I help you?"

If the Blu-ray player doesn't respond to this approach and swings back to talking about you, you will need to set a boundary. "Hey, this conversation just got disrespectful. I'm happy to continue when you're ready to show me your heart instead of telling me what's wrong with me."

Every respectful conversation needs one speaker and one listener at all times. Two Blu-ray players cannot communicate with one another. They will never know what movies they are trying to play until they hook up with a TV.

No one listening means there is no more conversation.

Creating Resolution—Choosing to Serve

Though it does require humility and vulnerability for the Blu-ray player to show the TV what is going on inside, the listening role is the true servant role in a respectful conversation. The listener affirms, "Right now, this conversation is about you and your needs. I'm here to help you figure them out and find a way to help you get them met." But in the end, the listener is really the winner. If I listen well, I will have two vital pieces of information—what you need and what I need to do. With these two pieces of information, I start to identify and take ownership of the problem and create an effective solution. If the husband of the hurting wife becomes a skilled listener, he is going to say, "Okay, she isn't saying that she needs flowers. She needs to feel loved. I take ownership for meeting that need. How can I serve her and show her I care? Hey honey, I got us a babysitter, a helicopter, and three nights at the beach! Let's go."

A skilled listener with a servant's heart is the deadliest weapon against the fear-bombs that threaten connection. And when you get two skilled listeners working together, watch out! They are ninjas at keeping fear away from their connection. As they engage in the mutual dance of going low and serving one another, they are going to remove all doubt that they care for one another. They are going to operate with the assumption, "You care about my needs and I care about your needs. We are going to invite and offer the exchange of truth every day in our relationship and stay connected." The more connection becomes the normal state of the relationship, the more quickly you will recognize signs of disconnection and be able to nip them—and their potentially deadly side effects—in the bud.

Not too long ago, Sheri and I disconnected over something. It was a remarkable experience because we both noticed how strange it felt. Although we had spent years in disconnection at the beginning of our relationship, we had been connected for so long that it was blindingly obvious that something was not right. So we started a conversation:

"This has been going on for like an hour. Does that feel weird to you?"

"Yeah, it feels weird to me. I hate it."

"You want a cup of coffee?"

"Sure."

"You want to sit on the couch with me?"

"Sure."

We knew the first item we had to tackle was reconnection. After that, we were able to resolve the issue very easily.

Most problems are solved in the momentum of protecting connection. But even when connecting does not solve a problem, it helps to keep the problem under control. For example, I recently had a 180-degree disagreement with an important leader in my life. We were like two freight trains moving in opposite directions, and it went on for months. After one hour of intense disagreement in a conflict-resolution meeting, I told him, "I'm afraid that this disagreement is going to injure our relationship."

"I'm never going to let that happen," he said.

To this day, he and I disagree strongly about something very important to both of us, but we protect our relationship. Together, we keep elevating our relationship above that issue in our hearts and minds. This affects how I treat him, how I talk about him, and how I talk to him. I refuse to let our disagreement intimidate me into moving away from him. I know that if I can prioritize connection in the midst of conflict, I am going to have something even more powerful to hold on to down the road.

So what can you take away from this chapter? Well, first of all, get started on your relational connection fitness plan. Get off the couch and start strengthening the cords of connection. Start respectful conversations by clarifying that you care deeply about the other person's needs. Then, send and receive clear messages. Don't participate in a conversation with someone who doesn't want to be respectful too. Choose to keep your love on, nuke fear, believe the best about people, and trust them to care. If they don't care, forgive them. Move toward those you love even when it hurts.

Section Three

BOUNDARIES

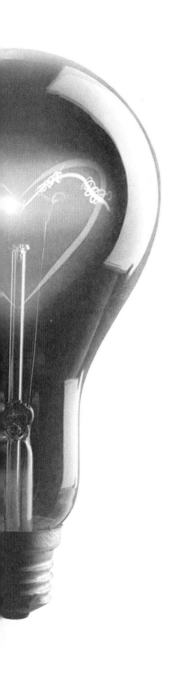

Chapter Eight

LEVELS OF INTIMACY

My friends Bob and Linda used to live like many well-meaning, good-hearted people do. And for the longest time, they couldn't figure out why their lives were always stressful, financially strained, and in relational survival mode.

Bob has a great talent for fixing cars, and always helped his friends out with their cars for free, even though he couldn't really afford it. Right before his little girl's seventh birthday party, he got a call from a friend saying that the car he fixed for free the previous weekend had broken down *again*. The friend begged Bob to come right away because he had to get somewhere ASAP. Bob kissed his little girl on the head and went to work on the car. After returning home late that night, he and Linda had another argument over how his friends and their car problems seemed to be more important than their family. But Bob couldn't figure out why using his talent to help people could be a problem. He saw it as his ministry.

Meanwhile, Linda had two friends whose daughters were getting married. Neither could afford to buy clothes for the bridal parties. Linda is a really good seamstress, so she offered to sew all of the dresses for both weddings for free. She sewed nonstop for two months. She missed a piano recital and a Little League championship game because she was running out of time to finish the project. Her commitments to help her friends brought a high level of stress into her life, but she powered through because that's what she was supposed to do. She was serving.

As for Bob and Linda's kids, well, they constantly heard their stressed-out, financially strapped, unavailable parents say, "This is ministry, kids." But the lesson they were learning was that "ministry" prioritizes the needs of strangers before everyone in the family.

Bob and Linda were not practicing "ministry." They were practicing a life without healthy boundaries. They were on the road to destroy their relationships with each other, their children, and eventually those they were trying to serve, because they did not know how to establish and protect appropriate levels of intimacy in their lives.

Levels of Intimacy

This might be news to you, but not everyone should have the same access to you.

You are responsible to manage different levels of intimacy, responsibility, influence, and trust with people in your life. Likewise, you are responsible to honor the different levels of access and influence others allow you to have in their lives. These levels are absolutely righteous, healthy, normal, and good. It is supposed to be like this! It has to be like this. When we expect that we should all have equal access to one another, we are setting ourselves up to violate and be violated.

For many Christians, this is difficult to grasp. We have core values of honor, love for the poor, serving others, laying down our lives, and being the "hands and feet of Jesus." It's easy to think that it is spiritual to offer all people unlimited access to our lives. But everyone who tries to do this eventually discovers that it is not sustainable, healthy, or spiritual…at all.

LEVELS OF INTIMACY 8

Here's an idea of what happens when you don't set boundaries around the levels of access and intimacy with people in your life. Say that you have been married for a while and have a few kids and a dog. Your husband comes to you and says, "Honey, Buster is cold sleeping out on the back porch. Do you think he could stay in here with us tonight?" You hesitate because you don't want one night with a 200-pound bullmastiff in your room to turn into every night. But since you don't want to upset your husband, you agree.

The next night, he asks, "Honey, little Joey is having nightmares again. Can he sleep in here with us? It will just be for one night."

> *To see the pattern for the Christian life, we must look at Jesus.*

A few weeks later, you have Buster, little Joey, not-so-little Suzie, and the pet gerbil all sleeping in your room. Not too long after that, your husband asks if his brother can borrow a few hundred dollars to pay off a debt. Suzie goes on an outreach and meets Debbie, who was homeless (until she moved into your house). And your husband's brother's crack-addicted friend is now knocking on your door asking for more money to pay off the debt he owes.

Hello?

This is not a good Christian life. This is a panic attack!

To see the pattern for the Christian life, we must look at Jesus. When we do, we see that Jesus prioritized certain relationships over others. He did not offer the same level of access and intimacy to everyone around Him. First and foremost, His primary allegiance was always to the Father. At twelve years old, He was already about His Father's business.[1] Everything Jesus did revolved around prioritizing that core relationship above all others. After the Father, the Gospels indicate that Jesus' closest relationships were with the twelve disciples. These were the people He partnered with, traveled with, taught, trained, and trusted. Within that group, He was especially closest to Peter, James, and John. They were privileged to share incredible revelations, encounters, and conversations with Jesus that no one else did. And of those three, we know that John was the one Jesus loved, the one He charged with taking over His role as Mary's son.[2]

The twelve, the three, and the one—this is the picture Jesus gave us of how many relationships we have the capacity to cultivate, and how to prioritize them according to levels of intimacy.

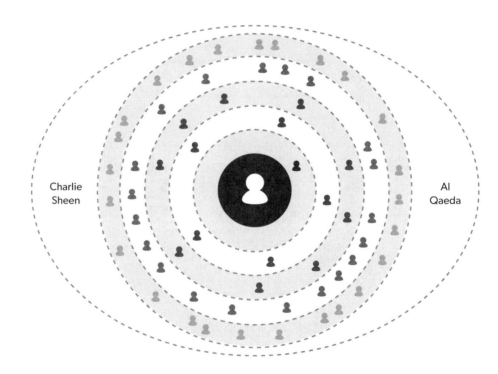

Charlie Sheen

Al Qaeda

This is a little diagram I created to illustrate the levels of intimacy we need to cultivate and protect with boundaries. The innermost circle is your core. Some people like to call this the "God Spot," because He's the only person who belongs at the core of your heart and spirit. Nobody else knows you and loves you like Jesus, nobody else deserves your heart's primary allegiance and worship, and nobody should hold the place of influence He holds in your life.

The next level of intimacy is for your most intimate human relationship, your deepest soul tie. *Only one person* is going to fit into that spot. If you are married, this should be your spouse. If you are unmarried, this person could be a friend, a parent, a sibling, or even a business partner. When you do get married, you'll face a delicate transition as you move the person who has been on that level back a circle or two and let your spouse take his or her place. This might be uncomfortable, but it must be done.

For example, say you are divorced or widowed and have allowed your children to occupy your innermost circle of intimacy. If you remarry and say, "I just want you to know that my children will always be most important to me," then you are effectively putting your spouse in submission to your children. This will not work out very well.

The further out we go in the circles of intimacy, the more people can fit in them. The next circle contains people like your kids and grandkids, followed by your closest friends. Heading out further, you have good friends, then co-workers, and then acquaintances. Keep going and you find people in the same geographic location, and finally the rest of the human race.

Yes, you are called to love "all people," but that doesn't mean that all people have access to your core. You may be called to pray for someone in Hollywood like Charlie Sheen or a group of people that feel scary, like Al Qaeda. Praying for them does not mean that you will allow them into your core circle. It's your job to manage your life so that you can offer the people in your inmost circles appropriate access to your core.

Sadly, sometimes people in our inner circle hurt or scare us very seriously and are unwilling to clean up the mess they made. If that happens, we must move them out to a place of access that they can handle. Some people who once held the "most intimate" place in our lives may find themselves out in the Al Qaeda sphere. We can keep our love on toward them, but it may be a very long time before we ever have them over for dinner.

Boundaries Around Levels of Intimacy

The level of intimacy people have in my life determines how much of myself I will offer them when they pull on the relationship. If I am chatting with someone from church for the first time and he tells me that the engine in his car blew up, I am probably going to give my sympathies and offer to pray with him for provision.

If I have interacted with the person a few times and know him a little, I will probably say, "Oh I am so sorry. Here is the number to my mechanic."

If one of my good friends comes to me with the woes of an exploding engine, I may toss him my keys and say, "Here, borrow my car until you can get your car fixed. Take your time."

If my daughter or one of my sons comes to me and says, "Dad, my engine just blew up." I will pull out my checkbook to cover the repairs.

And finally, if Sheri comes to me, there is no doubt in my mind that I am talking with the person who will be picking out the color of our next car. Because she is my most intimate human relationship, I am willing to put *all* my time, money, energy, and resources toward helping her with her problem. After Jesus, she is my greatest priority, and has greatest access to my life.

As a Christian minister, I have hundreds of people going in and out of the outer circles of my life. I have never had a conversation with most of them, but because I have influenced their life in some way, they feel like they have a connection with me. I have had countless people walk up and say, "Hey, remember me?" I think to myself, "No," but I smile and talk with them for a few minutes. I don't put up a boundary that says, "Don't talk to me unless you know me personally," but I also don't pretend that I can be something for that person I will never be. I love lots of people through my ministry. I counsel them, pray with them, laugh with them, and cry with them. But that's it. They don't get the bulk of my time, attention, or money. They don't get to know my heart and influence my decisions. After our few hours together, I leave those people at church and go home to my family and close friends.

It often surprises people when they find out that my name, address, and phone number are all in the phone book. Many people have advised me to change this, but I am okay with it because every one of these technological devices we call phones have incredible features called caller ID and voicemail. If you call me and your last name isn't Silk or Serpell (my married daughter's last time), you will most likely go to voicemail. I will decide upon hearing your voice whether to respond to you right now or wait until later. You will never be responsible to manage my time at home. That is my job. I give people a level of access to me by having my number in the phone book, but I have a boundary that I am under no obligation to answer or even call you back. I didn't set this boundary either to offend or please you; I did it to manage my priorities at my house.

> *I didn't set this boundary either to offend or please you.*

Do people ever try to demand more from me than I have decided to offer at their level of intimacy? Sure. This is where I have to honor my boundaries and make sure that I do not start treating someone on the outer circle like I treat one of my kids. As soon as I do, I am threatening my relationship with my kids, because they're the ones who rightfully belong on that level. Although I genuinely care about people's needs, I know that I have limited resources with which to actually meet them, and I have committed those resources to my closest relationships.

If I start pulling out of my son's account to meet the needs of a stranger, or out of my wife's account to meet the needs of my kids, I am violating the priority of my core connections.

Of course, because I have now invested consistently in my closest relationships for decades, it is pretty easy to honor the boundaries I have set around them. As their value has increased in my life, other things have become less and less capable of competing with that value. I don't feel remotely pressured to hand over my checkbook when an acquaintance comes to me with a car problem. I don't struggle with guilt over ignoring a phone call when I'm spending time with my wife.

This is how boundaries work. You say "yes" to something, which necessarily means saying "no" to everything else. At first, it may be a challenge to hold on to your "yes" as all the things you said "no" to present themselves and say, "Really? Why not?" But if you consistently set a firm boundary around your "yes," eventually the things you said "no" to don't present themselves to you as viable options. It becomes a lifestyle to live within your boundaries.

You'll be glad to know that Bob and Linda rescued their family from "ministry" burnout and began incorporating boundaries to protect their "yes" to their family before other people. Bob stopped working for free and started paying off his debt. Linda stopped sewing during her free time and now makes it to games, recitals, and a weekly date night with Bob. These changes have transformed the dynamic of their family. The kids feel loved, safe, and prioritized—and so do Bob and Linda.

Yes, people were upset with them for communicating that they had other priorities. Bob and Linda endured accusations that they were not very good friends. But by now they don't really care. Bob still helps out a friend every now and then, and Linda has volunteered to do a few alterations, but all in moderation. No longer consistently drained, they can actually minister to the hurting and needy. Their time with the Lord, their connection to each other, and their connection with their children has translated to a peaceful, connected, intentional lifestyle that they do not plan to change anytime soon.

Jesus Set Boundaries

Some people mistakenly think Jesus is like them—a whacked-out, co-dependent person at the mercy of everybody's needs. If we truly want to live the Christian life Jesus modeled, then we need to pay attention to the fact that He regularly set boundaries with needy people. For example,

Luke 8 records the story of Jesus raising Jairus' daughter from the dead.[3]

When the story begins, Jesus has just encountered a whole crowd of people who have been waiting a long time and desperately need something from Him. They know He has the resources and ability to meet their needs, and He has a track record of meeting people's needs. Somehow, Jairus makes it to the front of the crowd and asks Jesus to come heal his little girl. And Jesus makes a decision. He says, "Yes."

That "yes," in that moment, was also a "no" to a bunch of other people who all needed healing too.

Really? Jesus actually said "no" to a bunch of desperately needy people?

You bet He did. It's right there in the Bible.

Yes, we know that Jesus healed all who came to Him on many occasions (see Matthew 4:24, 8:16, 12:15). But in every case, it was because of His choice. This fact is particularly highlighted in the story of blind Bartimaeus.[4] When he hears that Jesus is walking past him, Bartimaeus starts yelling, "Jesus, Son of David, have mercy on me!" The disciples get irritated and tell him to be quiet, but he just gets louder, "Jesus, Son of David, have mercy on me!"

Jesus turns to Bart and asks, "What is it that you want?"

I can imagine Bart wasn't sure about this question. He was probably wondering, *Isn't it obvious? Is Jesus blind too?*

"My sight."

Jesus says, "Okay, here you go."

Bartimaeus asked and Jesus responded with an answer: "Yes." But Jesus' "yes" was not driven by Bartimaeus' need. Ultimately, Jesus said "yes" to every person He healed, and "no" at times to other people (though of course, this "no" was not necessarily a permanent "no" but a "not now") because He had dedicated His life to one big "yes." And that was to live out of complete oneness and partnership with His Father—to do what His Father was doing, say what His Father was saying, and be about His business.

The Big Yes

Jesus modeled the big "yes" that is to define our lives. I know for a fact that I would never have been able to make and keep the boundaries I have set around the relationships in my life if I had not said "yes" to that primary relationship with Jesus. If you don't prioritize your relationship with God, then your God Spot will end up with a human being in it.

That, my friend, is idolatry.

Many powerless people have allowed their spouse or someone else to scoot into that spot, and it puts their priorities, their resources, and their relationships out of whack. Their boundaries disappear. Soon, their kids are controlling their life, their marriage is falling apart, and before they know it, they're trying to escape it all by having an affair or taking up some ridiculous hobby or addiction. They end up as powerless, scared, and manipulative people who exploit relationships in order to survive them.

Conversely, putting God first in our lives won't compete with our human relationships. It will protect them, because one of God's top priorities in His relationship with us is teaching us how to love the people He has put in our lives. Keeping God in your God Spot keeps you connected to the Holy Spirit's incredible resources of wisdom and understanding to define your relational priorities and boundaries. He's going to show you who you're supposed to be, with whom you are supposed to be connecting, and how to build and protect those connections. He's also the Spirit of power, love, and self-control who enables you to follow through on your "yes" to these relationships.

Will there be challenges to keeping God in our God Spot and holding on to the big "yes"? Will there be things that try to compete with our value for Him, tempt us to violate our boundaries, and give away to others what only He deserves?

Absolutely.

The enemy wants to use these tests to distract us and ruin our lives. But God will use these tests to make us powerful. Likewise, it is powerful when we choose God above all other options, circumstances, feelings, and desires—especially when this choice is uncomfortable. Through the Gospel, God has made one thing abundantly clear. The big "yes" He asks of us is only what He has already given to us.

He created us with a God Spot because He has given us access to the deepest spot in His heart. He has placed the highest value on us, and His priority is nothing less than giving us all that He is. Saying "yes" to Him means saying "yes" to experiencing the incredible reality of His love for us. And the more we experience it, the easier it gets to live within the boundaries that keep Him as the priority in our lives and protect the priorities He defines for our relationships.

Chapter Nine

GUIDELINES FOR SETTING LIMITS

A few years ago, Suburban Auto Group came out with those hilarious "trunk monkey" commercials. A man is sitting in his car. He just made the mistake of honking at a truck driven by a huge, scary-looking guy. The scary guy has parked his truck, gotten out, and is banging on the honker's window roaring insults and threats.

Terrified, the man in the car grips his steering wheel, staring straight ahead, trying to ignore the thug until he goes away. Then he finds a piece of paper and plasters it against to the window in an attempt to block out the bad guy.

Finally, he remembers—he has a trunk monkey button!

He pushes it and the trunk pops open. Out jumps the trunk monkey, wielding a crow bar, and knocks out the scary trucker. The monkey high-fives the man in the car and jumps back in the trunk.

The first time I saw this commercial, I laughed hysterically. Who hasn't at one time or another wished they had something like a trunk monkey? How great would it be to push a button and have someone else handle all the upset, hurt, scared, needy people who try to pressure, intimidate, and manipulate you?

Alas, trunk monkeys only exist in commercials.

But for some reason, I still happen to encounter a lot of people who seem to believe that one day, a trunk monkey button is magically going to appear on the dashboard of their car. Instead of acting like powerful people and setting limits in their relationships, they continue to sit there, waiting for their problems to go away and letting other people roll over them.

This is how people end up in that destructive triangulation dynamic I described in Chapter 1. The commercial portrays triangulation brilliantly. You have three players—the powerless victim sitting in his car, the scary bad guy trying to intimidate the victim into compliance, and the monkey rescuer leaping to defend the victim. It's a perfect circle of control—the bad guy controls the victim, the victim controls the rescuer, and the rescuer controls the bad guy. But who wins in the end? The bad guy who is knocked unconscious? The monkey rescuer who has to go back and live in the trunk until called for? Or the victim who drives away, traumatized and not one bit more powerful or safe than he was before he unleashed his rescuer?

> ## 1. Learn to require respect in the relationship.

No one wins when you choose to be powerless against your problems. You only create more problems. In real life, unleashing a monkey who hits people with a crowbar is going to land you with a lawsuit. You destroy your relationships when you refuse to take responsibility to confront issues and set limits.

We all must accept the reality that the world we live in is filled with genuinely scary things and people who are hazardous to our health and relationships. Our longtime mortal enemies—the world, the flesh, and the devil—continue to wage their campaign to destroy our connections with God and one another. Not one of us will pass through life without encountering their threats and attacks.

However, that war has already been won. Sin and death, the barriers to our connection with God, are defeated. Nothing can turn off God's love for us or separate us from it. God's purpose in allowing us to face our enemies is to give us opportunities to rise up as true sons and daughters, capable of making powerful choices to turn our love on and keep it on, no matter what.

Nothing less than our eternal destiny is at stake as we learn to fight for our connections, manage our levels of intimacy, and set healthy boundaries around our lives and relationships! So let's give up the powerless search for trunk monkeys and start going after the exhilarating journey of learning to set our own limits and confront our own problems.

Taking Care of Yourself

Your life is a gift from God to you. It has infinite value to Him, which He communicates to you in all the many ways He loves you. God is always sending you love messages. If you feel that He does not love you, odds are, you have stopped opening your mail.

I spoke to a young man recently who told me he did not feel God's presence anymore. I asked him if he had recently been offended.

"Well, yeah," he answered. "At my old church. I got really hurt."

"Okay," I said, "Here is what I suggest. Clean up your forgiveness. That is most likely the key factor in why you are not feeling love. He hasn't changed. You have."

The young man dealt with his bitterness, and what do you know? He was able to reconnect with God's presence and feel His love again.

Do whatever you need to do so you can receive His love for you. The more you receive His love, the more you will learn to value your life as He does. The process of receiving God's value for your life is what anchors you in setting healthy boundaries.

Powerlessness, irresponsibility, and lack of boundaries are all rooted in failing to value your life as you should. Conversely, honoring God's value for your life will lead you to be responsible for protecting it and cultivating it.

After God created the world, He planted a garden "and put [Adam] in the garden of Eden to tend and keep it." [1] This is a picture of each of our lives. God has given all of us a garden to tend. He plants trees in it, and sends the sun and rain to make them grow. But we are the ones who have the responsibility to care for the trees and the right to enjoy their fruit. No one else has that responsibility. Only by being diligent in *managing what is ours* will we reap a harvest that will nourish us and give us something good to offer others.

Healthy relationships grow between people who have embraced their individual responsibility to tend their own gardens. Yes, both come to the relationship with needs, and participate in meeting one another's needs. But it is a simple economic principle that each of them must be healthy and fruitful in order to continue offering resources to one another to meet each other's needs. You have to take care of yourself before you can take care of someone else.

If you have ever been on a plane, you have been subjected to the flight attendants' spiel about what to do if the cabin loses pressure. They explain that oxygen masks will fall from the ceiling and show you how to put them on. Every time, they remind you that if you are traveling with a child or someone else in need of assistance, *you must be sure to put your mask on before you try to help anyone else.* The implication is clear. If you don't take care of yourself, then you won't be able to care for anyone else. You'll be lying unconscious in the aisle.

The lesson of the oxygen mask exposes the flawed thinking many people have about what it means to serve and love others. For some reason, people think that taking care of yourself means being selfish.

Yes, it's true that you can cultivate your garden and then choose to keep all your fruit to yourself. I know people who wrongly use boundaries to be independent and withhold their lives from others instead of using them to protect their ability to sustain fruitfulness, generosity, and the exchange of life in covenant relationships. Self-protection is not a good motivation for taking care of yourself, and will create problems in your relationships.

2. Tell others what you're going to do instead of telling them what they have to do.

But you will create just as many problems if you don't tend your garden. You're going to have to get food from somewhere, and it will have to be someone else's food. Not taking care of yourself actually puts you in the powerless position of trying to get other people to meet your needs without being able to offer anything in return. This is a setup for an unhealthy, selfish relationship.

If you truly want to be loving and unselfish, you will take the time and effort to get your garden producing the best fruit possible so you can offer something valuable to others. You will invest in learning all there is to know about the garden God has given you—from your physical, emotional, mental, and spiritual health to your education, talents, gifts, callings, finances, relationships, and more—and how to make it flourish. And as you share your life with others, you will be doing what you need to do to protect and sustain your garden's productivity so that your health and the health of your relationships are not threatened.

Consumers

The more you respect the value of your own life by cultivating your garden, the more you will create an atmosphere of respect around you. When people see how you care for your garden and taste the good fruit of your life, their words and behavior should demonstrate that they recognize your value. If they don't recognize the value of your life and what you have to offer, then you know that you cannot be in relationship with them. The only people you want to connect yourself with are those who respect the value of your life and their own lives. Only then will your relationships be based on mutual respect and shared fruitfulness.

The people you need to be able to set boundaries with are the people who recognize the value of your life, but want to relate to you as *consumers*. They are attracted to you and the good things you have to offer, but they are not offering much from their garden to you. These people may be good people who act polite and ask for things nicely. They may be people you find attractive and want to impress so much that you feel tempted to offer up yourself for their consumption. Or they may be aggressive, selfish users who use intimidation and manipulation to bleed you. You need a plan for dealing with all kinds of consumers who come into your garden.

As my grandchildren were growing up, we liked to watch the movie *Finding Nemo*. It is the story of a clownfish named Marlin who goes on a journey to find his son, Nemo, in the oceans off the shores of Australia. In one of the scenes, Marlin and his companion Dory wind up near the ship docks. Hundreds of seagulls are flying around saying, "Mine, mine, mine," as they peck at food, the fish, and each other. Each seagull is completely unaware of the fact that every other seagull is saying the same thing. They are each taking whatever they can get in small pieces.

Seagull consumers are challenging to deal with because they are only asking for one little peck at a time. It's easy to let people like this close to us and give them the benefit of the doubt as they peck at our resources. "Oh, you just need a few minutes, okay. A few dollars, okay. A meal, okay." It all seems harmless until you realize, "Man, I spent six hours today handling all these little requests. Did I really give away $100 this week?"

You get a bunch of these seagulls all pecking little pieces away from your life, and before you know it, your garden will look like a pumpkin patch in November. It can be difficult to set boundaries with these types of consumers, because each one of them may only be doing minimal damage. But if you want to preserve the health of your garden, you absolutely *must* set limits for how many people you allow to get near enough to you to take pecks, and how many pecks you allow them to take.

There's a learning process involved in identifying the types of consumers that want a piece of your life and the kind of boundaries you need to set with them. When we lived in Weaverville, everyone had eight-foot, chain-link fences around their gardens to keep out the deer. If bunnies are your problem, then you probably only need a few feet of chicken wire. Whatever the necessary boundary, its purpose is to protect the value of what is inside the garden and keep consumers out.

The beautiful thing is that when you have the necessary boundary in place, you don't need to treat consumers like the enemy. If your garden has a fence, you can choose to throw some fruit over for a deer or offer a carrot to a bunny. When you have healthy boundaries, you stay in control of the resources of your life and manage them toward your priorities.

The Trap of Bitterness

If you cannot set boundaries with consumers, you are going to be exploited.

Being exploited is not pretty. We all have had different experiences with being taken advantage of by consumers. But what really matters is how we respond to these experiences. Will we forgive the offense and become powerful people who can protect and share our resources more effectively? Or will we agree with the disrespect that was shown us, take on a victim mentality and allow people to continue to devalue our lives until we are fully exploited?

People commonly end up fully exploited by becoming offended, bitter, and resentful toward consumers. Many wounded, traumatized people fall into this trap. The seagulls have pecked them to the bone, and they are hurting. Or maybe a friend has been very needy for a long time and you feel absolutely sucked dry after being the only one pouring into the relationship. One way or another, healthy boundaries were not set. And instead of taking responsibility for this and setting a boundary, you blame the seagulls and the friend for his problems and become bitter.

If you are bitter toward someone, every encounter with that person will jar that place of wounding and offense, agitating your pain. He or she may do the very same things that other people in your life are doing, but for some reason, when he or she does it, it feels like battery acid being thrown in your eyes. Eventually, you will explode in anger. One day, you will go to the beach with a shotgun and kill as many seagulls as you can. Or you will blow up at your friend, tell him or her how horrible he or she is, and yell, "Here's a boundary—stay away from me!"

Trust me, this is not a good way to set limits. After choosing bitterness, you will still be wounded, and on top of that you will have destroyed relationships and will still have absolutely no guarantee that you will not be exploited again. The vicious merry-go-round will go around and around until you get so bitter that you turn your love off completely.

Setting Limits In Close Relationships

What happens when we wind up with a coworker, family member, spouse, or best friend who decides to start acting like a consumer? As we saw in the last chapter, these people get to demand more from us because of the access we have given them—they are in the inner circles of intimacy. If they start pulling on our connection to meet their needs and we don't ever pull back by setting a boundary or asking for them to meet our needs in return, then we are going to be dragging on the ground pretty quickly. The fruitfulness of our garden can diminish at an alarming rate if we do not know how to set boundaries with our close relationships.

You know what? Jesus set boundaries with His best friends.

One of my favorite examples of this is when Jesus explains to the disciples that He is going to suffer trial, condemnation, and the cross, and then be raised from the dead. Peter essentially responds, "You can't go to the cross. We've got a good thing going on here. This has been three years of awesomeness!"

Jesus spins around on His heel and says, "Get behind Me, Satan!" [2]

Whoa! Jesus called Peter *Satan*. Why? Because, in that moment, He was talking to Satan, the one who ultimately opposed His destiny.

"You're not in agreement with God on this one, Peter," He went on to explain. "You are not mindful of the things of God, but the things of men." [3]

Jesus had to set a limit with Peter because he was threatening Jesus' first priority to do His Father's will.

Obviously, Peter was not intentionally trying to get Jesus to disobey God. But this story illustrates a danger we all must face. The closer a relationship is to your God Spot, the greater the chance that the relationship could compete with Him as your top priority. It all depends on whether or not you decide to listen to the fear of man. If the needs and wishes of your spouse, kids, or best friend start to gain a greater hold on your heart's affections and begin to define your priorities and choices, then you betray your allegiance to God. When you do this, you are actually aligning with Satan just as Peter did by elevating the things of men above the things of God. His priorities alone must define your life and choices, not the needs and choices of people—even the people you care about most.

Similarly, you must be careful about demanding or allowing others to put you in their God Spot and defining their priorities and boundaries. You can encourage, invite, support, and enjoy others as they take responsibility to cultivate their gardens and value the life God has given them. But you must never take over that responsibility. Respecting the line between your life and the lives of others communicate love to them. You are saying, "You get to be a whole person in this relationship."

People who take responsibility for other people's lives and try to become their personal trunk monkeys are not loving. They are selfishly consuming another person's life and preventing him or her from becoming a powerful, responsible, whole person in the relationship. This is what codependency looks like. Parents with children who have drug or alcohol problems most often fall into this trap. Refusing to confront and hold their children accountable, they live in a state of denial as to why these things are happening, and in turn they enable the addict to continue a destructive life. Codependency is driven by the agreement that I will work harder on your problem and your life than you do. That is not love.

It can be one of the most difficult things in the world to set a boundary with someone in your inner circle who is breaking your heart with his or her choices. But if you want to protect your relationship with that person, you must be powerful enough to hold up your commitment to pursue the standard of respect in your interactions. If the person is consuming too much of your garden for you to stay healthy, you will also need to limit the access the person has in your life, while still keeping your love on.

If my son or daughter has a drug addiction or some other out-of-control lifestyle, I am responsible for setting up boundaries so they do not consume my time, energy, and resources beyond a healthy level. Before they lost control, I could trust them to take anything from my fridge. But now, they may decide to take my TV and computer so they can buy drugs. If necessary, I will change the locks on the house and inform them that I will call the police if they stop by when I am not there. I still love them, but I have set up a necessary boundary to protect the rest of my family, myself, and ultimately, my relationship with them.

What Are You Going to Do?

As the saying goes, the best defense is a good offense. You're simply not going to be successful at setting boundaries if most of your time is spent defending yourself against the requests and demands of consumers. A good plan of offense is making sure your focus is fixed on cultivating the resources of your garden and directing the bulk of those resources toward mutually beneficial, healthy relationships.

In order to carry out this offensive strategy, you need to get really good at telling yourself and others what you are going to do.

"I'm going to go spend time with the Lord right now."

"I've committed that evening to my wife."

"I'm taking my kids on a hike that day."

"Saturdays are my day to read and study."

These are all statements that set boundaries and tell people, "This is where I'm pointing my resources. I love you, but I can't give you what you are asking from me at this moment because I have other priorities."

As a powerful person, you always want to be focused on what you have the power to control—yourself. You also want your choices to be defined by the priorities you have committed yourself to, not by the choices of other people.

When you tell someone what you are going to do, ask yourself, "Am I making this choice to protect my priorities? Am I making sure that I am only telling this person what I will do and not telling them what they need to do? Will I honestly be okay no matter what he does?" It's important to be able to answer "yes" to these questions if you want to maintain a successful offense in keeping your boundaries.

I get to practice telling people what I am going to do all the time. Everything from crisis situations to mild requests land in my voicemail on a regular basis, and I get to be powerful as I respond to them.

For example, a while back I got a call from a guy at church. "Pastor, it's George. My wife left me last night. She told me in a note on the fridge. I think she is serious this time. I need to see you right away!"

Clearly, George was coming to me with a need he thought I could meet—a need he felt was very urgent. However, the needs of others do not control my choices; my priorities do. As it happens, one of my priorities is helping people who are going through relational crises, so I knew I wanted to help George with his need. But I also had to balance that priority with my other priorities. I had already told my son that I would play basketball with him the evening that George called me. The next day was our family day. Family *always* takes precedence over ministry in my life. So I made a choice. I would wait till I could look at my calendar in two days, see what I had open for George, and call him back.

Two days later, calendar ready, I made the call. "Hey there, George. I am calling you back. How are you doing?"

"Good Lord," came the distressed voice on the other end. "Were you sick or in the hospital? It took you two days to call me back!"

> ## 3. Remember that people believe your actions more than they believe your words.

"No, George. Actually, I was playing basketball with my son. The game went long and then I needed to spend time with my family. What can I do for you?"

"I don't know, but I need to get in to see you. I have to see you. Can I come in right now?"

"Well, you can come anytime you want. I will be glad to meet with you on the nineteenth of this month."

"The nineteenth? That is like two weeks away!"

"I know."

"But you're a pastor! I have to see you right away! I just need five minutes!"

"I have an hour on the nineteenth. That is what I will do for you."

"But the note said that she won't come back until I see you!"

"Probably so. I will let you finish this conversation with my assistant who can set up that meeting for you on the nineteenth. Bye."

I never told George what he could or could not do. I told him what I would do, without making excuses, apologies, or any attempts to convince him that my choice was right. I didn't need him to like the choice or agree with it. I didn't care if he was offended by it. I simply laid my offer on the table and left him to consider it.

This is what it looks like to let powerful choices communicate boundaries to people.

The Ability to Say "No"

In order to be consistent in telling ourselves what to do, we need to be able to do two other things. First, we need to be able to follow through on what we say we will do. And second, we need to be able to say what we will not do. Every "yes" needs to be backed up with action and a clear "no" to everything else.

As we saw in the last chapter, Jesus was able to say "no" when He needed to. Another amazing account highlighting Jesus' power to choose is found in Mark. In this passage, Jesus sends the disciples across the Sea of Galilee into a windstorm while He spends time with the Father. Then, in the middle of the night, Jesus sees the disciples in the boat rowing away, desperately fighting the wind. He starts walking across the Sea and easily catches up to the boat. Inexplicably, the Bible says He "would have passed them by." [4]

What is that about? Jesus' buddies are struggling in the boat, and He is going to pass them by? Why would He do that? Well, it was one of His options. He didn't have to go to them. He did go to them after they cried out to Him. But this verse makes it clear that Jesus had a choice. He could have said "no" to the disciples. He was able to say "yes" because He was also capable of saying "no."

So many people say "yes" to things they really want to say "no" to, which makes their choices powerless, not powerful. This can easily happen when people don't wait to find out what they're choosing when they choose it. These situations may go something like this:

"Hey Danny, you want to help me move?"

"Sure. Yeah, I can do that."

"Tomorrow?"

"Uh, my son has a baseball game in the morning."

"No problem. How about at 6:00AM? You busy then?"

"It's my day off, so I wasn't planning on getting up that early. But sure."

"Can we borrow your truck? We don't have one."

"Yeah, uh, sure."

"Great. Can you fill it up with gas because I don't have any money?"

"Okay."

You can just feel the anxiety of a trapped victim growing as this conversation progresses. If we want to make powerful choices, then we need to find out just what we are choosing, and we also need to know that we can say "no" as well as "yes." See how the conversation goes when we do that:

"Hey, Danny. Want to help me move?"

"I can't because I am practicing boundaries today."

"Why?"

"So that when I do help everybody else this week, I will know that I can say 'no.'"

When you start telling people what you're going to do and what you're not going to do and follow through on both, people come to believe what you say. Your words have weight. The first time that you turn around and walk out of a disrespectful conversation, you will probably surprise and maybe even offend the other person. But it will also set a standard for being in a relationship with you. If the person you walked out on wants to keep you in the room during your next conversation, then he will manage himself to honor your standard.

I know a woman who decided she would no longer contribute to any disrespectful conversation ever again. The next time she and her husband had a disagreement that led into rage and intimidation, she stopped and announced, "I'll be glad to finish this conversation when it becomes respectful. I can see you are upset. As long as it stays respectful, I'll stay."

He continued to explode. She walked out.

He was stunned at first, then angry. He felt powerless and punished; he sat and fumed in anger. His wife waited a full hour before she returned to the room. She had remained calm and self-controlled, because she had a genuine desire to resolve the conflict. She came and asked him if he wanted to have the conversation again.

After seeing his wife consistently behave the same way in their various disagreements, this husband became convinced that she really was never going to participate in a disrespectful conversation. He also began to believe that if she could control herself, so could he. If at any time she said, "I'll be happy to have this conversation if it stays respectful," he started to adjust his tone and choice of words so he could keep her in the room while they worked out the conflict.

This couple now has a new standard for conversation when they have a conflict, a standard they both prefer. Good communication and healthy boundaries gave these two adults what they needed to stay powerful and maintain their connection. They have more trust, honor, and love for one another. Their conflicts are resolved in a way where both feel safe—but only because they were both willing to change.

The more others encounter us honoring the boundaries we have set for our lives, the more they will know that they can trust us with their lives. Setting and honoring boundaries is essential to creating a relational culture of respect, honor, trust, and love in our connections with people.

Chapter Ten

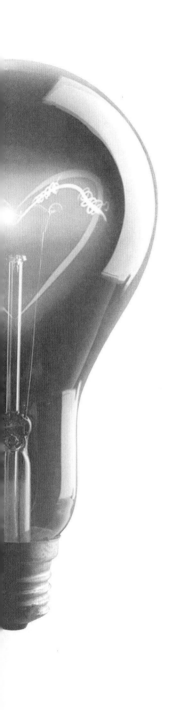

DID YOU LEARN TO LOVE?

Love is changing my city—Redding, California. Each week, members of the church where I am on staff and students of the ministry school go out to bless Redding with prayer and practical ministry for the homeless and addicts on the street, people living in halfway homes, jail inmates, and poverty-stricken families. They pick up trash, pull weeds, and scrub away graffiti. If there is a need in the city, our students can't wait to volunteer to fill it. Our leaders are also actively involved in pursuing our community leaders so we can build connection with them and learn where we can best strengthen the health of our city.

Redding used to be a little wary of our church's outreaches, but they have come to receive them and gratefully acknowledge the benefits we are offering. Instead of trying to get people to come to our meetings and conform to us, we are going out into the community and blessing it. We are turning our love on and asking our city, "What do you need?" We are building trust by meeting those needs. Our goal is not to create distance with the "world," but to remove disconnection and fear wherever we find it. We are responding with love to the brokenness we encounter in people's lives and inviting them to become healthy, powerful, and free along with us. And people are responding. They feel loved. Trust, honor, respect, cooperation, and connection are beginning to flourish in the relationships with our community.

The Sin Problem

Many of the Church's evangelistic efforts have been directed toward getting people into a building where they can be cleaned up and reformed out of their sinful lifestyles. Unfortunately, the methods used for this "clean up" process are nothing more than the old "rattlesnake" tools of religion—fear, control, and punishment. Once people get "saved," they find out that despite what they've heard about the cross, everyone in church is still freaked out by sin. It's hard to go out and love sinners like Jesus did when you're still afraid of your own sin. This is why many churches are failing to make a significant impact in their cities.

The Church simply must get deeply in touch with what the Gospel actually means in regard to how we are now to relate to God and man. Jesus invited people into a connection with Him, not a religious reform program. He showed up in the midst of our brokenness with compassion and healing, shocking everyone by how fearless He was about keeping His love on with sinners. Jesus didn't create distance with broken people; He created connection. But this shouldn't surprise us, because we know that His entire mission was to finally remove sin—the source of all relational disconnection—through the cross.

First John 2:1-2 states, "When he served as a sacrifice for our sins, [Jesus] solved the sin problem for good—not only ours, but the whole world's."[1] Other translations use the word "propitiation"— "He Himself is the propitiation for our sins…"[2] Propitiation is the completely satisfying sacrifice that closes the gap between God and His children. Only Jesus Christ could serve as this sacrifice, and He did. *He solved the problem of sin.* He solved it for everyone, for good. It doesn't matter who has or has not "prayed the prayer." Sin has been handled, and everyone has access to the Father.

Yet for some reason, so many Christians believe that people can only be forgiven and saved at the beginning of their relationship with God. "It doesn't matter what you did," we tell new converts, "because you are washed by the Blood. You were once Scarlet O'Hara and now you are Snow White. You are clean." And so they come in, grateful to be accepted. But soon they discover that this acceptance isn't unconditional, by any stretch of the imagination. Instead what they hear is, "Okay, now that you are here, now that you are clean, you can never make a mess ever again. We are keeping track. This is a holy place. There is no sin in here."

If you happen to burst this bubble of delusion by making a mess, then you are punished—usually, by people turning their love off and disconnecting from you. Or, your home group leader or pastor or some random church lady will tell you to knock it off and get your act together so the image of "spotless" can be maintained for the public. You quickly learn that if you want to preserve "relationship" in the church, then you cannot show people the truth of who you are. You must submit to control by hiding, performing, and agreeing.

Church leaders have to pretend they don't ever sin. If you ever expect to move up the ladder of church leadership, then you have to become pretty fabulous at keeping secrets. "This next level here, this is where we put you in charge of stuff. Now, this one right *here* is when you have a toilet in your house, but you have to act like you never use it. And people at this level *here*, well…they don't use a toilet. Finally, *this* level would be senior leadership. That's when they actually come to your house and remove the toilet."

Maintaining the illusion that absolutely no sin exists at the top of the ladder creates a ridiculous gap between regular people, who sin, and leaders, who supposedly do not. It turns leaders into liars, because they are not allowed to be real people anymore. This only sets them up for isolation and a fall.

I am in the people business, and I know people. There are people on the ground level and there are people ten stories up. I am a person. Ask my wife—she will confirm that with a resounding, "Yes!" Being in the people business and being afraid of sin is like being a rancher and being afraid of manure. Imagine a rancher saying, "Oh yeah, we taught the cows to walk around with their tails between their legs. We have officially created a manure-free farm right here and our cows are permanently clean!" Trust me, manure-free cows go against nature. And eventually one of them will, well…KABOOM!

That is what happens in the Church. We create a false expectation based on an illusion, because we are so afraid of people's mistakes. Then our leaders occasionally just go KABOOM and get their mess all over everything. But we never say, "Oh yeah, now I get it. You're a person too. Welcome to the ranch." We say, in horror and shock, "See, that's why we are afraid of people right there. Now, everybody is hurt and smelly."

Have you ever read the Bible? Believe it or not, it is full of stories about people who made big messes! There's stuff in there that you definitely don't want your children to read. But unlike us, God never once pretended that these mess-makers weren't going to blow it. We imagine that God was surprised and disappointed when Adam and Eve ate the fruit. "Really! I can't believe you guys did this! How could you? How could you make such a big mess—now everything is ruined!" But we are mistaken. God knew exactly what He was getting into when He went into the people business. He has never been afraid of manure. In fact, He has the most blindingly brilliant plan for dealing with manure. The cross separates us from our mess every time, no matter how big.

> *The cross separates us from our mess every time, no matter how big.*

Love, Love, Love

By solving the sin problem, Jesus created a safe place—the safest place in the world—for us to be loved, known, accepted, and forgiven. But He gives us one big requirement if we want to live and flourish in this safe place of relationship with Him:

"This is My commandment, that you love one another as I have loved you." [3]

If we're not obeying Christ's command to love one another, then we simply don't know Him or have much of a relationship with Him at all. As John wrote, "My dear children, let's not just talk about love; let's practice real love. This is the only way we'll know we're living truly, living in God's reality." [4]

A lot of people think that if they're using their spiritual gifts, they must have a relationship with God. But gifts can be used outside of connection. Gifts can be used without love. The sign that you are in relationship with Jesus is that you love people—period. I have crossed paths with so many people who say that they have an amazing relationship with Jesus, but in reality, all they have are some amazing gifts from Jesus. And I know this is by looking at how they love. They dance with flags, paint prophetic pictures, and pray all the time in their prayer caves, but they don't know how to open their hearts to another person and build an intimate connection. They don't know how to know or be known. They have retreated from relationships, thinking that they can be "spiritual" without them. Unfortunately, this won't work. Our spiritual calling is nothing less than to love and to be loved by God and people. Our spiritual training and growth can only occur in the context of relationship.

Our spiritual training and growth can only occur in the context of relationship.

The whole nature of relationship is that you cannot control it. All you can control is your free choice to love others and receive their love. When you make this choice, freedom grows and fear goes. The sign that you really have love in your relationships is that you and the people around you are free and are not scared. Free people are going to tell you the truth. They are going to make mistakes. That *will* test the relationship and the state of your heart. It will require you to grow up and become powerful. But the more powerful you become, the more you will be able to hold on to your connection with people and help them as they work through their truth and clean up their mess—just like Jesus does.

So...Did You?

I once heard a man tell his story about being struck by lightning— twice. He actually died, and believe it or not, ended up in heaven talking to God.

God didn't ask him, "Did you give all your money to the poor?" or "Did you raise the dead?"

Instead, He asked, "Did you learn to love?"

The man said, "No."

Then God gave him another shot at life.

I think that we should pay close attention to the question, "Did you learn to love?" This is the question. That is the one thing you are responsible for. It is the only thing that God cannot work out for you.

No matter what miraculous things God is doing around you and through you, you must never lose sight of this priority. All the signs, wonders, gifts, and supernatural events in the world do not prove that you are connected heart-to-heart with God. Jesus warned about the last days when people will come to Him and ask, "Didn't I prophesy the paint off the wall? Didn't I do amazing things in your Name?" and hear Him say, "I never knew you." [5] Do you want Jesus to know you? Do you want to know Him? Then love Him and love others. The Bible couldn't be more clear about this:

"But if anyone loves God, this one is known by Him." [6]

"Beloved, let us love one another, for love is of God; and everyone who loves is born of God and knows God. He who does not love does not know God, for God is love." [7]

People who really know God can do shocking things. They can do powerful things. *They can love people that many would declare unforgiveable and impossible to love.*

A woman recently told me, "Danny, I wanted to thank you. Two years ago, you took the time out of your day to call me while you were at the airport between flights. My nephew raped my daughter. I was about to go into court when we talked. You said that I needed to keep my heart open to my nephew and to keep my love on. You also said that my daughter would follow our lead of forgiveness and reconciliation. I had already listened to a message you had given about keeping your love on, and my heart wanted to love. But my mommy claws were about to come out. You gave me the clarity I needed to be okay and I chose the right way to protect my daughter's heart."

"That event could have destroyed my family forever. But we chose to love. We created boundaries and loved with our whole hearts. There were lots of 'God moments' throughout the trial and they continued to come afterward. We have had a family gathering since then and I look at him now without hating him in my heart. We are not afraid, because we chose to love. Fear never took hold. I am now addicted to this full, open heart of love. It has made me know how safe and powerful I truly am. And our daughter has followed our lead. She has forgiven him and loves well. She has not forgotten, but she truly loves."

When Jesus asks this woman if she learned to love, she will be able to answer, "Yes."

What about you? How are you answering this question right now in your relationships with God and others?

Love That Can Go To Hell and Back

One of the most important opportunities to answer this question in our family came through our relationship with Sheri's older brother, Ted. Ted struggled for a long time and made messes everywhere. Drugs were a huge part of his life—heroin, meth, you name it. Everywhere Ted went was a disaster zone.

Ted's girlfriend gave birth to his son while she was in prison. At the time, Ted was living with us, and he and Sheri flew down to Southern California to pick up his newborn baby. Ted began raising his son in our home and walking with the Lord. We fell in love with his little boy.

Sadly, a few years later, within a few months of his girlfriend getting out of prison, Ted went back into the drug scene. Sheri and I visited him on occasion in his ramshackle drug home and tried to talk to him. He had no electricity and no running water. The carpet was burnt from candles falling over and starting fires while everyone was passed out. Ted's son, then four years old, would often run unsupervised up and down the street in their rotten neighborhood.

During one visit with Ted, who looked worse that he ever had, his son brought his car seat out of the house and put it in our car. But we couldn't take him with us—he was not our son. It was absolutely heart-rending.

Much later, Ted told us he remembered that day and saw that there had been a spiritual battle going on. "It was like you were an angel trying to rescue me," he said. "But I was in so much darkness that I didn't want anything to do with you."

A few weeks after that visit, the authorities arrested Ted and his son went into foster care. He was absolutely out of control. We had to do something. We became foster parents and took our nephew home.

At that time, I had been a foster care social worker for several years. But I had never seen anything like my nephew. He manifested demons every day. On one occasion, he turned to Sheri, who was holding onto him, and said, "I'm going to cut your head off and spit down your neck."

We did numerous deliverances on this little boy over the course of a year. Gradually, he calmed down and began to behave normally.

Wonderfully, Ted eventually reconnected with Jesus and got healed. He was able to get his boy and life back. Every year, Ted gets a sobriety coin from Narcotics Anonymous. He has given every one of these coins to Sheri. Recently, Ted came over and handed Sheri his ten-year coin from NA. He says that no one has ever loved him like she loved him.

My wife's relationship with her brother has been filled with craziness. I can't think of anybody who has been as challenging to keep close to the family as Uncle Ted during those tough times. We watched him go to Hell and back…and we kept our love on the whole time. Now, Uncle Ted would take a bullet for us, and his son is doing just fine—in fact, he is doing wonderfully.

Bigger Hearts

David wrote, "I will run the course of Your commandments, for You shall enlarge my heart." [8] If we're going to keep the one big commandment He gave us—to love as He loves—then we need bigger hearts. If we'll let Him, I think God will make us like Secretariat, that freakishly fast champion racehorse who blew contenders away with his shocking, unprecedented stamina. After his death, veterinarians discovered the secret to this horse's incredible power. Secretariat had a heart nearly three times the size of an average horse's heart—an estimated twenty-two pounds. Just imagine what would happen if a bunch of Christians started walking around with hearts three times as powerful and loving as anyone else around them. People might actually start believing that God is real.

It's time for the world to see a Church who can keep her love on. It's time for the sons and daughters of God to mature into a company of powerful people who know how to walk in freedom, practice intimacy and vulnerability, clean up our messes, and invite people around us to become powerful, free lovers. It's time for those who bear the Name of Jesus to become famous for carrying His huge heart—that absolutely fearless heart of love that pursues connection with broken sinners. This is how the world will know we know Him.

So ask God to give you a twenty-two pound heart—His heart. Then turn your love on, and *keep your love on, no matter what.*

I'll leave you with this declaration to make over your relationships:

I know the Spirit of power and love are at work in me.

I can love at all times through Christ who strengthens me.

I am courageous with my love.

I am powerful to control myself no matter what others choose to believe or do.

My goal is connection, not distance.

I will tell others about me and let them tell me about them.

I matter and so do you.

I clearly and honestly express what I am feeling and what I need to feel.

I listen well to what others are feeling and what they need to feel.

I communicate my value and priorities by expecting respect.

I show respect by listening well and honoring the boundaries of others.

I keep my love on and chase fear out of my most vital relationships.

In Jesus' name, Amen!

Endnotes

Chapter 1

1   John 15:16 NKJV

2   For more on Sozo, visit www.bethelsozo.com.

Chapter 3

1   2 Corinthians 3:17 NKJV

2   2 Timothy 1:7 NKJV

3   1 John 4:18 NIV

4   Psalm 32:8 NKJV

Chapter 4

1   Proverbs 9:1 NKJV

2   1 Corinthians 13:13 NKJV

3   Steven Pressfield and Jeremy Leven, *The Legend of Bagger Vance*. DVD. Directed by Robert Redford. Universal City, CA: DreamWorks, 2000

4   Proverbs 29:18 KJV

5   Hebrews 12:2 NKJV

Chapter 5

1   Mathew 12:34 NKJV

Chapter 6

1   Mathew 18:6 NKJV

2   See Erik Erikson's theory of psychosocial development.
(http://en.wikipedia.org/wiki/Erikson's_stages_of_psychosocial_development)

Chapter 7

1   Ecclesiastes 4:9-12 NIV

2   John 6:56 NKJV

Chapter 8

1   Luke 2:49 NKJV

2   John 13:23, 19:26 NKJV

3   Luke 8:42 NKJV

4   Mark 10:46-52 NKJV

Chapter 9

1   Genesis 2:15 NKJV

2   Matthew 16:23 NKJV

3   Matthew 16:23b NKJV

4   Mark 6:48 NKJV

Chapter 10

1   1 John 2:1-2 The Message

2   1 John 2:2 NKJV

3   John 15:12 NKJV

4   1 John 3:18-19 The Message

5   Matthew 7:23 NKJV

6   1 Corinthians 8:3 NKJV

7   1 John 4:7-8 NKJV

8   Psalm 119:32 NKJV

Other Loving on Purpose Resources

Love is a choice.
Learn to love on purpose at **lovingonpurpose.com**

"His stories will capture your heart, his wisdom will astonish you, and his life will change you forever."

Kris Vallotton
SENIOR ASSOCIATE PASTOR OF BETHEL CHURCH,
REDDING, CA

A FRESH, FREEDOM-BASED
PERSPECTIVE ON PARENTING

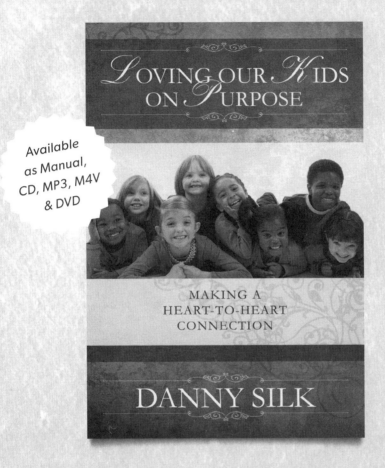

Available as Manual, CD, MP3, M4V & DVD

Loving Our Kids On Purpose brings fresh perspective to the age-old role of parenting. Through teaching, storytelling and humor, Danny shares his personal family stories as well as numerous experiences he's had helping other families. You will learn to:

- Protect your heart-to-heart connection with your children

- Teach your children to manage increasing levels of freedom

- Replace the tools of intimidation and control

- Create a safe place for children to build confidence and personal responsibility

View this and more at lovingonpurpose.com

READY FOR MARRIAGE? DANNY EQUIPS YOU FOR THE "BIG" CONVERSATION

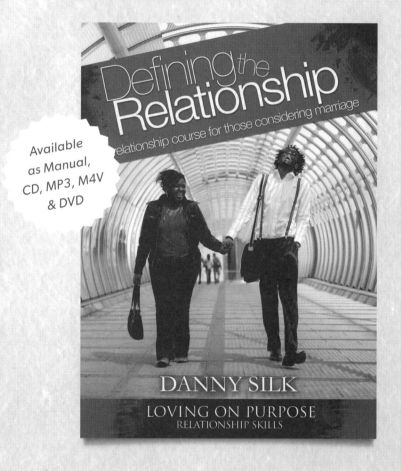

Many Christian couples come to a point where they must "Define their Relationship." In this series, Danny's comedic style of teaching will inspire, challenge, and bring couples into a serious reality check about their decision toward marriage. The goal of this series is to impart COURAGE—the courage to either push through the rugged realities of a loving relationship or the courage to walk away. Whether you are single, dating, or already engaged, this course will teach you how to love on purpose.

View this and more at lovingonpurpose.com

WITNESS THE KINGDOM AS YOU
LEARN TO LIVE IN HONOR

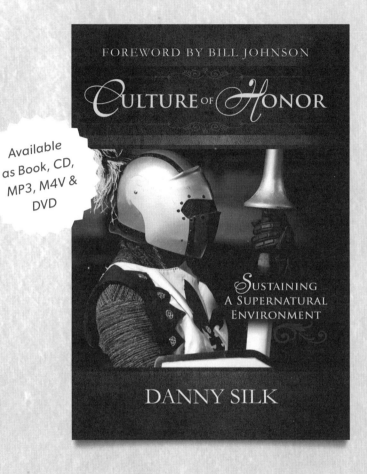

In this powerful, revelation-packed book, Danny Silk describes the significant paradigm shift in church life, government, and relationships that has created and sustained the revival culture at Bethel Church in Redding, California. Through many relevant and true-life stories, the church is revealed as a place of freedom, respect, empowerment, and healthy discipline (not punishment). Culture of Honor challenges the status quo of church leadership structure and presents a refreshing view of the five-fold ministry.

View this and more at lovingonpurpose.com

WHAT IS HONOR AND HOW DO YOU PRACTICE IT?

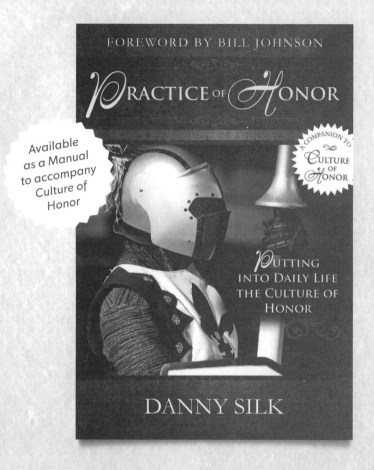

The Practice of Honor manual is a practical resource for those who have read the Culture of Honor by Danny Silk and for leaders, individuals, or those who desire to learn how to cultivate a culture of honor in their sphere of influence. In some realms, honor is something to defend...The Practice of Honor may require a significant paradigm shift in your thinking. Based on the revival culture of Bethel Church in Redding, California, it is a template to help any leader develop an environment that brings out the very best in people. It is a recipe for introducing the Spirit of God—His freedom—and how to host and embrace that freedom as a community of believers.